Heads Up

how to anticipate business surprises and seize opportunities first

Kenneth G. McGee
Gartner, Inc.

HARVARD BUSINESS SCHOOL PRESS
BOSTON, MASSACHUSETTS

No part of this publication may be reproduced, stored in, or introduced into a retrieval system, or transmitted, in any form, or by any means (electronic, mechanical, photocopying, recording, or otherwise), without the prior permission of the publisher. Requests for permission should be directed to permissions@hbsp.harvard.edu, or mailed to Permissions, Harvard Business School Publishing, 60 Harvard Way, Boston, Massachusetts 02163.

Library of Congress Cataloging-in-Publication Data

McGee, Kenneth G.
    Heads up : how to anticipate business surprises and seize
    opportunities first.
        p. cm.
    Includes bibliographical references and index.
        ISBN 1-59139-299-3 (alk. paper)
        1. Business forecasting. 2. Real-time data processing. 3. Business
    intelligence. 4. Decision-making.
    HD30.27+

                                                            2003019056

The paper used in this publication meets the requirements of the American National Standard for Permanence of Paper for Publications and Documents in Libraries and Archives Z39.48-1992.

To Bonnie, Aly, and Tim

contents

acknowledgments

I believe it is very difficult to truly appreciate how much of other people's work goes into writing a book until you actually write a book yourself. I know I certainly did not until I started my own literary journey with this book. It seems unfair that a body of work that relies upon the talents and influences of so many other people should have only one name on the cover. Thanks to these acknowledgments, I can set the record straight as to where real credit should be directed.

First, I wish to thank Bob Knapp, executive vice president, strategic planning, at Gartner. I am eternally grateful that he encouraged me to write this book, which has brought a wonderful completeness to five years of research and given me a life experience that I will treasure always.

I am also grateful to Dean Daniels, senior vice president, Gartner Research and News. I will long remember his many kindnesses and words of encouragement as well as his wise guidance and counsel throughout the entire project.

Heather Pemberton Levy, publisher of Gartner Press, was a remarkable source of strength and guidance throughout the project. When I first met her I did not know what a publisher did. While I may still be a bit unclear on that point, I now know that there would be no book without Heather's tireless dedication to the thousands of details that go into transforming an idea into a book.

Then there is Tim Ogden, who stood shoulder to shoulder with me every step of the way. Tim served as editor, researcher, negotiator, and confidant as well as a hundred other roles and never, never, never lost his sense of humor. Tim's abilities gave my words life. There simply would not have been a book without Tim. He may be the most undiscovered jewel at Gartner, and I hope this work finally makes his talents and abilities more widely known. But most of all I will remember his kindness, his intellect, and his strength of character. Tim quietly became a hero of mine a few years ago when he took a sabbatical to serve as a volunteer providing humanitarian assistance during a famine in Africa. I never thought that the twists and turns at Gartner would allow us to work so closely together. In my life I have met few people like Tim, but when I do, I realize that angels do walk among us on this earth. Thank you so much, Tim.

There are a few others who also deserve specific mention: Dave Levy, who researched many of the examples in this book and was certainly a key player; Fred LaSenna, for emergency help with graphics; Susan Barry, Gartner Press's literary agent, who helped pull the ideas together into a compelling form; and Jacque Murphy, my editor at Harvard, for her patience with a first-time author.

I would like to thank the entire Gartner research community, both Core Research and GartnerG2. These are rigorous research environments that demand much of their research analysts. The rigor of the research effort that I followed while writing this book was guided by my desire to meet the standards they have all set. I especially want to thank Mark Raskino, David Flint, Tom Austin, Neil MacDonald, Tom Bittman, Donna Scott, and Gartner's current and former research fellows for their efforts on my behalf and toward advancing the ideas of

Real-Time Enterprises. In my career, the title of *research analyst* has been the title of which I have been most proud. I hope this work justifies my continued usage of that cherished title.

From a personal perspective, I want to thank my wife, Bonnie, for being my biggest supporter and for her unfailing assistance throughout this project. She was always the first one to hear the ideas and theories when they were in their earliest and most unrefined states and was invaluable in adding life to them. When I searched for examples, I first turned to her. This book truly has her thoughts and ideas throughout its pages. To my daughter, Aly, and my son, Tim, thank you for allowing me to work on this project during the days, nights, weekends, birthdays, and many holidays that were required to finish the book. Most of all, I will never forget the proud looks and encouraging wishes you both gave me throughout this journey.

I also want to thank my mother, Eileen; Peggy, Tom, Jenny, Terry, Eileen, Bob, Amanda, Ethan, Bill, Elaine, Robert, and all my other family members; as well as neighbors and friends for the extremely kind and generous words of encouragement they bestowed upon me throughout this project. I only wish my late father could have seen this book, and so much more.

Finally, to Charles Randall. More than thirty years ago I was driving a farm tractor that was hauling a trailer full of hay behind me. While going up a steep hill I jerked the tractor forward, snapping the chain that connected the tractor with the trailer of hay that many others had just loaded. As I watched the trailer pick up speed as it raced backwards down the hill toward a small creek, I saw how my error was about to ruin the hard work of others. The trailer finally stopped, thankfully without toppling over. Charlie then calmly told me to go and hitch the trailer up again and to take it back up the hill. Still shaking, I refused because I was afraid that I would make the same mistake again. He quietly and gently insisted that I go retrieve the trailer anyway, and I did. I finally delivered the trailer safe and sound with cargo and the hard work of others intact, with my confidence somewhat restored. That is just one of the many lessons Charlie taught me that helped me to write this book.

introduction:
there's always warning

The year was 1900.

The first sign of trouble occurred on August 28. Despite being only twenty-four hours old, a massive storm already had its first victim. A ship off the Cape Verde Islands was being tossed about in heavy seas in twenty-four- to thirty-six-mile-per-hour winds.[1] For the next few days the storm would move across the Atlantic, growing in intensity moment by moment while going virtually undetected. On the afternoon of September 8, the Category 4 hurricane passed directly over Galveston, Texas, destroying the city and killing 8,000 people. To this day, the Galveston hurricane of 1900 is the worst natural disaster in U.S. history.

Even though storm warnings had been posted four days prior to the utter destruction of Galveston, people there did not know the approaching storm was actually a hurricane until it was too late. Galveston's weather forecaster Isaac Cline wrote in his account of the storm later that month:

> The usual signs which herald the approach of hurricanes were not present in this case. The brick-dust sky was not in evidence to the smallest degree. This feature, which has been distinctly observed in other storms that have occurred in this section, was carefully watched for, both on the evening of the 7th and the morning of the 8th.[2]

By the time anyone knew the monstrous hurricane was descending on them, it was too late to react. All people could do was watch in horror as the city was leveled and so many of its residents killed. The people of Galveston (and the rest of the world) would have to wait decades before meteorologists would possess the technologies that could accurately detect approaching hurricanes.

The year was 2000.

For many people, the first sign of trouble occurred on March 13. Like the Galveston hurricane a hundred years earlier, a great storm, this time a financial hurricane, started wreaking havoc on stock valuations and thereby on mutual funds and retirement portfolios. However, unlike the Galveston hurricane, where the early warnings came just weeks before the disaster, the end of the meteoric rise in the NASDAQ Composite Index arrived after many *years* of warnings. Unfortunately, most people simply did not see the warning signs that the great Internet investment-hype bubble would burst and therefore failed to take appropriate measures to protect their assets. During the next thirteen months, investors watched in horror as the market ravaged the value of investment portfolios and destroyed the hopes and dreams of millions of people. (See figure I-1 showing the change in market capitalization of NYSE and NASDAQ exchanges.)

FIGURE I-1

The market capitalization of the NYSE and NASDAQ indices dropped dramatically between 2000 and 2002.

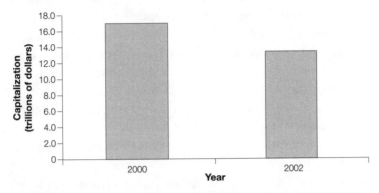

Source: 2000 NYSE data based on 2,862 listed companies (data from New York Stock Exchange, *New York Stock Exchange Fact Book: Year In Review 2000,* <http://nyse.com/pdfs/01_SUMMARY2000REVIEW.pdf>, 5); 2002 NYSE data based on 2,783 listed companies (data from New York Stock Exchange, *New York Stock Exchange Annual Report,* <http://www.nyse.com/pdfs/2002ar_NYSE-2002.pdf>, 43); 2000 NASDAQ data based on 4,734 listed companies; 2002 NASDAQ data based on 3,663 listed companies (data from Judith Chase, Vice President and Director, Securities Research, Securities Industry Association, telephone interview by author, 13 March 2003).

We Know More About the Status of Hurricanes Than We Do About the Status of Companies

Today we cannot envision a scenario where an approaching hurricane could make landfall in the United States without being detected well in advance by the National Weather Service. A sophisticated network of supercomputers and land and sea sensors work together with Geostationary Operational Environmental Satellites to constantly monitor emerging weather patterns in real time so that forecasters may issue weather advisories when warranted.

But when comparing the state of real-time monitoring of weather patterns with real-time monitoring in business, the business world has roughly the same capability as hurricane forecasting had in 1900. Managers may hope for a sign in the sky to allow them to know the current situation, as weather forecaster

Isaac Cline did, but more often than not they are unaware of changes in the environment around them until it is too late to take action. Product managers have to wait far too long before receiving important information about changes in customer demand. Marketing professionals must wait weeks or longer to determine the effectiveness of their recently launched campaigns. Executives everywhere must guess what new product will be received favorably by customers, when the opportune time is to launch the product, and how to maximize the product's impact on customers. Investors interested in monitoring the health of the companies they invest in have little more to rely on than four measurements per year, when those companies are compelled by regulation to report quarterly earnings.

While the astonishing reductions in corporate value that began in 2000—consensus estimates hover at $7 trillion—may be staggering in their sheer size, they are also woefully lacking in their ability to convey the enormously harmful impact they have had and will have on millions of people for many years to come. Since the dramatic reductions in stock prices started in 2000, pension funds have lost staggering amounts of value, 401K plans have been decimated, and saving strategies have been undermined, leaving millions of people to reassess how they will fund their own retirements, medical expense needs, children's educations, and so on.

Consider a few simple examples. As of spring 2003, the Dow Jones Industrial Average was at the same level that it was seven years before. Making some significant assumptions,[3] a family who began saving for a house seven years ago would have the cash for a down payment on a $300,000 house rather than a $480,000 house. If the family had been saving for retirement, the impact would be roughly $150,000, more than five years of retirement income for the average American (inflation adjusted). The effects of the burst bubble will certainly be passed on to children. Consider how many high school graduates have decided not to apply to Ivy League or other private colleges because their families can no longer afford the tuition. Each of these examples says nothing of the tens if not hundreds of thousands of people who have been out of work for six months or more, due at least in part to the bursting of the Internet bubble. While no lives were directly lost as a result of this stock market hurricane, surely the cumulative effects on families all across the United States can be called devastating.

The fact that the bursting of the Internet bubble came as such a surprise to so many has, unfortunately, not led to a widespread inquiry as to how such a "storm" could have arrived unexpectedly. In fact, the majority of actions taken, with the possible exception of New York State attorney general Eliot Spitzer's settlement with investment banks,[4] are focused only on punishing fraud committed by a very few companies. The total economic damage caused by WorldCom and Enron combined would be only a rounding error in the $7 trillion mentioned earlier. The Internet bubble burst long before Enron and other corporate scandals came to light.

The frightening truth that must be dealt with is that the bursting of the Internet bubble was simply the daily occurrences of the business world writ large. Business "surprises" of all sizes occur with alarming frequency and take a considerable toll, without the press coverage of more profound and widespread failed investment events. Every day there are hundreds if not thousands of business "surprises." They are manifest most tangibly in missed earnings reports (called, of course, "surprises") at the end of a quarter, but they happen every day: Managers make critical business decisions with outdated and practically useless information leading to the surprises of missed opportunities at best or disastrous failures at worst for businesses, for managers, for employees, for the economy.

The aftermath of the Internet bubble bursting led me to wonder if there was a pattern that could be discerned that held for all business surprises, large and small.

To pursue this line of research I first looked at a number of "surprises" outside the world of business, such as the incident at Three Mile Island, the Buffalo Creek (West Virginia) flood, Aloha Airlines Flight 39, the Hilo (Hawaii) tidal wave, the Mount Saint Helens eruption, and the *Challenger* disaster. I quickly discovered that before every disaster I could find, there was always warning. I then turned my attention to the world of business. I limited the research on business surprises to events that had occurred in the last five years. Given the tremendous changes in technology, sourcing, globalization, and myriad other factors in the business environment, I felt that only very recent examples would be relevant to the investigation. Consequently, many of the examples cited are still "in progress"; further developments that change outcomes may occur, but I felt this was a necessary risk to ensure that the research was relevant to present circumstances.[5] In conducting the research I relied heavily on the public records and regulatory filings made by companies, such as quarterly and annual reports of operational and financial performance, court proceedings, and presentations to investors and analysts by company executives. Wherever possible I tried to conduct interviews with executives of the companies; most were quite willing to discuss the events in question, with a few understandable exceptions—many executives are all too happy to consign negative surprises to the past.

From this research, conducted with the aid of several colleagues, we arrived at a number of conclusions that ultimately led to this book and are presented in the following chapters. None is more central than this: *There is always warning before a business surprise takes place.*

Why Do We Allow Surprises to Happen?

The question that inevitably follows from this conclusion is: Why do we allow these surprises to happen? Why do we allow so much damage to occur, so many opportunities to be lost?

It is especially hard to understand why we continue to allow business surprises to occur when research shows that we react utterly differently to every other type of negative surprise in our public lives. In nonbusiness situations, we immediately assume that there were warning signs that someone should have noticed. Rather than acceding to surprises and allowing them to continue unabated, we take measurable steps to (1) determine what the warning signs were, (2) understand how the warning signs of the disaster were missed, and (3) ensure that these surprises don't happen again.

Let's look at our research on arguably the three disastrous surprises most indelibly inked in the American psyche to see what we can learn about business disasters.

Three Mile Island

On March 28, 1979, a pump that feeds a constant supply of water for the steam creation process failed in one of the two nuclear reactors at Three Mile Island (TMI), located near Harrisburg, Pennsylvania. Noticing the change in pressure that resulted, an operator opened a relief valve at the top of the water tank to bring the pressure back to acceptable levels, per operational guidelines. The relief valve needed to remain open for just thirteen seconds; however, the relief valve failed to close properly and no technician noticed. The valve remained open for two hours and twenty-two minutes. As a result, the pressure dropped well below the safe operating range, the core of the reactor nearly reached "meltdown" stage, and a large amount of radioactive material was released into the atmosphere.

A commission was quickly established by President Jimmy Carter to determine the cause of the accident. The commission studied the situation in detail and found a number of disturbing facts, not least of which was that no one should have been surprised that the relief valve at TMI did not close properly. Eighteen months earlier a similar failing of a relief valve had occurred at another reactor (located in Ohio) built by the same company that built the TMI reactors. Babcock & Wilcox engineers warned their superiors of the likelihood of the incident occurring at other plants, but no warnings on the valves were reported to TMI or any other reactor or utility.[6] The commission ultimately recommended changes in the operating procedures of plants and the Nuclear Regulatory Commission to ensure the proper flow of information from engineers and designers to operators.[7]

Space Shuttle Challenger

Most of us know the results of the presidential commission that was created immediately to investigate the shocking result of the launch of the Space Shuttle *Challenger* on January 28, 1986. The explosion was caused "by a failure in the joint between the two lower segments of the right Solid Rocket Motor. The specific failure was the destruction of the seals that are intended to prevent hot gases from leaking through the joint during the propellant burn of the rocket motor."[8]

The tragedy of the joint failure is magnified by the commission's discovery that the failure was expected, given the ambient temperature at launch. According to the report, engineers at the companies responsible for the shuttle and its rockets told NASA repeatedly that the O rings would fail, but the launch was carried out anyway.[9] The commission concluded: "If the decision makers had known all of the facts, it is highly unlikely that they would have decided to launch [the *Challenger* mission] on January 28, 1986."[10]

The commission recommended significant changes in the process NASA uses for approving launches. A similar commission convened after the *Columbia* disaster found, most tellingly, that the damage caused by insulation debris to the shuttle's wing integrity was suspected. As is now well known, NASA declined the opportunity to have the shuttle photographed in space to ascertain whether the engineers theories were correct. This time the commission is recommending changes to the way the shuttle safety program is run and to the way mission risks are assessed after take-off.

September 11, 2001

Of course, the tragedy of the *Challenger* has been superseded in our collective conscious by September 11, 2001. Without going into details that we all already know too well, let us just note that an investigation was launched to determine how such a horrible event had taken place seemingly without warning. In both the preliminary and final reports of the Joint Inquiry Staff of the Senate Select Committee that investigated the attacks, the senators concluded that while there was no specific evidence about the exact attacks, there was warning. The final report, released in July 2003, stated:

In short, for a variety of reasons, the Intelligence Community failed to capitalize on both the individual and collective significance of available information that appears relevant to the events of September 11. As a result, the Community missed opportunities to disrupt the September 11 plot by denying entry to or detaining would-be hijackers; to at least try to unravel the plot through surveillance and other investigative work within the United States; and, finally, to generate a heightened state of alert and thus harden the homeland against attack.[11]

As a result of the attacks, President George W. Bush created a new cabinet-level department, the Homeland Security Department, to bring together the appropriate resources and hopefully ensure that such communication breakdowns do not lead to another such surprise.

What Do We Learn?

What do the examples show us about how we generally treat surprises or unexpected events with negative consequences? First, and most important, there was clear warning of impending disaster in each case (a pattern that holds for virtually every public disaster on record). Second, in general, we do not assume that these events were unpreventable. In fact, we assume just the opposite: that there was in fact some way of preventing the surprise. Third, in each case, action was taken to investigate how the surprise might have been prevented. Specifically, in each case a task force conducted a thorough investigation into why the warning signs were not caught. Fourth, in each case, specific actions were recommended and are at least in the process of being taken to prevent similar surprises in the future.

Meanwhile in the business world, a cursory glance through the headlines during what is popularly known as "earnings season" (when most companies announce their quarterly earnings) will show that hundreds of those companies announce earnings different from what is expected, both positively and negatively, called "surprises." In the vast majority of cases, management of the company attributes the deviation from targets to an "unanticipated" or "surprise" event; for example, "There was unexpected weakness in the consumer sector." However, none of these announcements include an announcement by the CEO that he or she has commissioned a group to discover why the change from target was unanticipated—why advance warnings were missed—so that the downside can be avoided or the upside exploited to its maximum in the future. So again we must ask, Why do we treat business surprises differently?

Four Common Business Assumptions Must Be Changed

The answer to this question lies in four common assumptions that are unspoken yet very much a part of our subconscious programming as businesspeople. The only way to destroy these assumptions so that we can move on is to confront them head on.

Assumption 1: Business surprises are just a part of business reality.

Reality: For the first time ever, businesspeople have the potential to consistently detect opportunities and avoid disasters, thereby ending business surprises.

This is perhaps one of the most damaging assumptions because it prevents any effort to analyze how to end business surprises. It leads to an excessive focus on determining how to respond to unexpected conditions (a situation we'll look at in more detail in part 3) rather than ensuring that changes are not unexpected. The reason this assumption is so widely held is that for scores of generations, business surprises have indeed been a way a life. Today's labor force comprises history's first generation of businesspeople who can break this cycle of surprises and desperate responses. *For the first time ever, businesspeople have the potential to consistently detect opportunities and avoid disasters, thereby ending business surprises.* Businesspeople no longer have to endure the harmful effects of business surprises if they choose not to. But favorably exploiting the end of business surprises must begin with a fundamental change in the way people think about the present.

Assumption 2: The data needed to anticipate surprises just don't exist in the business world.

Reality: The data are there.

As recently as ten years ago this assumption may have been a valid objection. The current reality, however, is that the data are there, although they are often not in the hands of the right person (an idea we'll return to later). The data required began to be generated the first time a computer was used to speed up a task like payroll. But the ball really started rolling in the 1990s as organizations began focusing on two goals: (1) aligning people, procedures, and processes for maximum efficiency and quality and (2) applying technology to the "front office" rather than the "back office." Because of the vast investment in reengineering and total quality management (and their successors and imitators), many organizations today know far more than ever about their own workflows. They know what each individual is doing in the business process, be it taking an order, compiling a report, or driving a rivet. As technology has been applied to "front office" applications like sales and customer service, a whole new world of information has been created. Enterprises that have implemented call center applications know almost exactly how many customer service representatives they need taking phone calls at each hour of the day. Businesses that have implemented sales management systems know far more than in the past about how many dollars of orders must be in the individual sales person's pipeline to generate each actual dollar of recognized revenue. Gartner Dataquest estimates that more than 65 percent of companies with a hundred employees or more have implemented enterprisewide software that creates, collects, and processes operational data every moment of every day.[12] The bottom line in modern businesses is that *the data are there*.

Assumption 3: There is too much data.

Reality: Very little of the data available is actually necessary.

Hand in hand with assumption 2 goes the idea that there is so much data that no useful conclusions can be reached, a situation sometimes called "analysis paralysis." Certainly, at face value this contention would carry weight with anyone who has an e-mail address—or voicemail, for that matter. The volume of information pouring into all our "in boxes" is so much greater today than it was twenty years ago that it may be unquantifiable. However, as anyone with an e-mail address also understands, while there is a great deal of information available, *very little of the data available is actually necessary* to accomplish one's goals. Once you classify the possible information to be tracked by its priority, materiality, and other factors (concepts we'll look at in much more detail in chapter 2), you will find that no more than 5 percent of the available data is necessary to end business surprises as we know them.

Assumption 4: There's no way of anticipating events, so why try?

Reality: There is always warning.

Recall for a moment the examples of unanticipated events discussed earlier. In the investigations of each of these disasters, there is an indication that information that may have or definitively would have prevented the disaster was available before the event occurred. And this situation is not coincidental or rare. Nearly every investigation launched into a surprise or disaster has shown that evidence was available in advance: Pearl Harbor, the Buffalo Creek (West Virginia) flood, the Aldrich Ames spy case, the sinking of the *Titanic,* the Zeebrugge ferry disaster, Aloha Airlines Flight 243, and so on. The disastrous outcomes in all these cases were the result of decision makers basing decisions on information that was not current. In some cases the needed information was not being tracked; in others it was knowingly or unknowingly withheld from decision makers. Therefore, if information that would allow us to predict disasters is so often available outside the business world, why should we believe that business is any different? In fact, throughout this book you will find examples of companies who were the victims of surprises when information was available to allow the company to turn that event into an opportunity or mitigate the damage. Further, you'll see a number of examples of companies that have taken steps to see change as it happens and capitalize on it. In business, *there is always warning*.

Business Culture, Not Bad Managers, Is the Problem

These assumptions need to be stated not only to disprove them but also to show that the problem isn't bad managers. While certainly we can look at some of the examples and fault specific managers or individuals for their actions, that exercise misses the point. The problems that need to be dealt with are systemic— bad processes and bad culture. This means not the culture at a specific corporation but the culture of the entire business world; a culture that has become satisfied and complacent in using outdated and often irrelevant information when making decisions. It is time to change the prevailing culture and the processes that go along with it. Unlike many of the remedies proposed for the corporate accounting scandals, fixing this problem is not a regulatory or government oversight issue. It requires no new laws, changes to the criminal code, or any oversight boards. It requires only the concerted efforts of managers and executives to change the prevailing business culture and focus existing processes on getting the right information to the right individuals in real time.

Business surprises, the unexpected events that rule the business world every day, should not be surprises. The information that would allow managers to turn these currently unexpected events into opportunities is available. If managers and businesses focus on capturing and presenting certain material information in real time they can "predict the present" and put an end to the devastating consequences that follow in the footsteps of business surprises.

What This Book Will Do for You

This book is not about management or leadership styles. It is not about setting goals or teamwork or knowledge management. It is most definitely not about technology. This book is about improving every manager's ability to meet goals by ending surprises and detecting opportunities.

The purpose of this book is to prove that by far most of the business uncertainty we live with today is unnecessary; that the primarily negative "surprises" we have come to live with should in no way be surprises. Through the course of the book, you will see how the individual business manager can be the agent for change that brings about the end of surprises, bringing the manager no small gains in material prosperity and prestige.

In the following chapters, you'll be introduced to the concepts of predicting the present, real-time opportunity detection, and Real-Time Enterprises, and even more important, we'll look at a methodology for applying these concepts in your daily job. This methodology will help you determine which information is materially important, which business events warrant being captured and analyzed in real time, and how to prioritize the information flows to be monitored. Of course, the methodology will also help you to avoid processing a glut of meaningless information in a world already overloaded with data.

Once businesses overcome cultural hurdles and use real-time information, managers will decode trends and assess probable impacts before they occur. By doing so, they will devise appropriate strategies to capitalize on whatever is transpiring. As a result, they will become vital participants in bringing new productivity, efficiency, and profitability to their companies and growth to the overall economy. Individual managers making small changes that capitalize on opportunities and avoid disasters can have a huge impact on a company's success or failure. Individual managers who start thinking in terms of predicting the present and real-time opportunity detection can change the future of their companies. They will take the blinders off themselves and their corporate executives, officers, and directors with an unparalleled ability to see what is going on while events unfold.

This book is directed at every manager who is responsible for expenses or revenues. The concepts here are simple and specific and apply at every level of the corporation:

1. The data that can be used to avoid surprises, to capitalize on opportunities, and to make midcourse corrections already exist.

2. Although many businesspeople are concerned about "infoflood," the amount of data that is *material* is relatively small and can be determined.

3. Once material data are identified, they can be captured and monitored on a continuous basis.

4. Monitoring allows departments, business units, and entire corporations to see every day the progress they are making toward their goals—what we call predicting the present.

5. They can anticipate events and changes so that they can adjust tactics and strategies to ensure that goals are met, opportunities are maximized, and disasters are avoided— what we call real-time opportunity detection.

At a personal level, application of these concepts should mean unprecedented success at meeting targets and objectives, unprecedented improvements in productivity and efficiency, and with any luck, unprecedented upward mobility, especially when compared with peers who are not thinking in this way. *In short, rather than preparing the manager for uncertainty, this book will prepare the manager to drive out uncertainty and take control of the future of his job and her company.*

Identifying and Justifying Real-Time Information

Talk with employees, managers, or senior executives who have ever made a large business mistake, missed a huge business opportunity, or been overwhelmingly surprised by a business competitor, and they will be able to tell you what information they wish they had possessed before the mishap occurred. The capture and presentation of real-time information so that mishaps may be avoided, opportunities may be seized, and unpleasant surprises eliminated is what this book is all about.

But in a world that is already overwhelmed with a staggering abundance of information, how does one determine the correct information to monitor, capture, and analyze in real time? To resolve this question, we have developed real-time information "identification" and "justification" methodologies that will help employees and managers determine which specific information warrants real-time monitoring. By first evaluating a manager's goals and priorities, the Identification Model determines what information streams are most valuable, then determines whether obtaining these streams in real time is sufficient. The Justification Model then helps a manager determine whether the positive impact of the real-time information is worth the cost of obtaining and monitoring it by evaluating corporate vision and mission, current corporate priorities, the "materiality" of information, and finally corporate impact. These methodologies assist the manager in filtering out information that may initially appear to be vital but in fact is unrevealing and therefore unnecessary. After both models are employed, the manager can begin putting an end to today's all too common business surprises.

What's to Come

Part 1

In chapter 1, we delve into the core concepts of predicting the present and real-time opportunity detection and discuss the three types of business surprises. Then in chapter 2, we lay out the methodologies for determining the information you need to predict the present and begin detecting opportunities in real time.

Part 2

In part 2, we begin applying the methodology to real-world examples of the various types of business surprises. Chapter 3 looks at companies and an entire industry that were not monitoring the right information to predict the present and so were caught by surprise. In chapter 4, you'll see two companies that didn't have the right information in the right hands until too late; both had to announce a huge earnings "surprise." In chapter 5, we show five companies that are already enjoying the benefits of real-time opportunity detection today.

Part 3

Part 3 broadens the perspective from the individual manager to the overall corporation. Chapter 6 discusses the steps needed to take real-time opportunity detection to the corporate level, specifically how to truly become a Real-Time Enterprise. Chapter 7 points the spotlight on the changes in executive functions and governance needed to become and remain a Real-Time Enterprise. In chapter 8, we close by discussing the many changes that will ultimately be ushered in by Real-Time Enterprises, covering everything from marketing and information technology spending to monetary and fiscal policy.

ending business surprises

O N APRIL 11, 2002, General Electric's investors received a shock when company executives announced the company's first-quarter 2002 financial results. Wall Street's earnings-per-share expectations for GE in the first quarter were $0.35, but GE reported only $0.25 per share. By 4:00 P.M. that day, 79 million GE shares had been sold, the price had fallen 10 percent, and GE's market capitalization had dropped $34 billion dollars (see figure P-1)!

Certainly Jeff Immelt was not the only CEO to announce earnings less than what was expected by investors; scores of other CEOs joined him in announcing earnings "surprises" over the next few weeks. Experienced investors have come to expect such surprises and the impact they have on markets. Experienced managers have come to expect surprises that interfere with their ability to meet goals.

In the Introduction, we showed that there is always warning for every business surprise, and therefore the business sur-

FIGURE P-1

GE's market capitalization fell by $34 billion because of an earnings surprise.

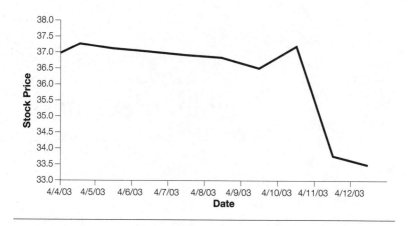

prises that are so common today need not be. In part 1 we will describe an idea we call *predicting the present*, which will begin the process of eliminating business surprises. Once we have established how predicting the present can offset or avoid harmful business surprises, we will describe three types of events (*surprise, suspected,* and *surmounted events*) to illustrate how real-time monitoring techniques can lead to a sustained environment we refer to as *real-time opportunity detection.*

Finally, part 1 will provide methodologies (real-time information Identification and Justification Models) that will enable business professionals to identify the specific information they need in real time to help ensure success in their current positions while significantly enhancing their chances to move on to greater responsibilities and rewards within their companies and careers.

1

turning business disasters into opportunities

. . . [the] voyage required a helm to grasp, a course to steer and a port to seek.
—Henry B. Adams

T HROUGHOUT THE AGES people of different cultures have both marveled at and scorned certain people's (often self-proclaimed) ability to predict the future. To this day a remarkable number of people still read and reread with reverence the quatrains of Nostradamus to determine whether the latest major event or catastrophe was actually foreseen by the famous sixteenth-century prognosticator. Even the most cynical among us still seem quite willing to turn attention each February to a silly ceremony in Pennsylvania where a groundhog and its shadow are used to predict whether spring will arrive soon or if winter will continue to keep millions in its cold grasp. Supermarket tabloids at the end of the year are covered with the latest revelations of the future; given their seemingly growing number, it would appear these issues of the publications are highly successful. Hundreds of thousands of investors scan the Web looking for reliable predictions of the future of certain stocks and investments. Predicting the future is something we all wish we could do.

Predicting the Present

This book is not about predicting the future. It's about something entirely different: *predicting the present.*

Predicting the present accurately describes how we understand the world around us. The idea behind the concept is similar to a principle of molecular physics, the Heisenberg Uncertainty Principle. The Uncertainty Principle states that it is impossible to know everything about a subatomic particle at the same time. Specifically, we cannot know both the position and the momentum of a particle simultaneously since measuring one of those parameters changes the other.[1] Physicists know that they can't know everything about the particles they study. The same is true of the way we interact with the world around us. We don't gather complete information about situations we encounter—we don't need to. We gather just enough for an intuitive leap to be made about the status of the big picture: predicting the present!

Predicting the present means taking certain raw empirical information, analyzing it, and determining its meaning and implications. When someone is outside in the middle of the day and glances at the sun to estimate the time, she is predicting the present. When a lost person pores over a road map trying to determine his current location so that he can take the correct exit to reach his intended destination, he is predicting the present. When a physician puts a patient through a battery of tests to determine the cause of the patient's illness, she is predicting the present. When a geologist sets off an explosion to take seismic readings in a search for oil deposits, he is predicting the present. In none of these situations does the individual have complete or comprehensive information about the situation. They simply have enough current information to make sound predictions of what that complete information would be at that moment.

The same principle applies in the business world. There are so many variables that affect products, markets, and internal operations that no individual manager can possibly know everything that's happening in a business at the same time. Any manager who tried to collect all operational data would find that the first piece of data had changed substantially by the time the last piece of data was collected. The reality is that we, as managers, don't need to know *all* the operational data to understand what the present situation is.

Herein lies the main cause of unnecessary and damaging business surprises. The pieces of information that are assembled to allow the business manager to make the intuitive leap about the big picture are so out of date that rather than predicting the present, most managers today are predicting the past. In essence, the manager is attempting to decide the best route to the office in the morning based on traffic reports from last month. So, just as predicting the present is not predicting the future (it does not answer the question "Where will we be at the end of the quarter?"), it is equally not predicting the past ("Where were we at the beginning of the quarter?"). Predicting the present is gathering enough information to answer the question "Where are we *right now* in meeting our corporate goals?"

Predicting the present doesn't change the manager's job; it changes the manager's ability to do the job *successfully*. Managers must still decide what the appropriate goals are and how best to reach those goals in the time frames specified. Managers must still choose strategies and make the right tactical decisions to execute those strategies. But just as a captain of a ship can make changes in course or speed to ensure reaching the desired port at the right time, the manager who has the current information necessary to predict the present will have a superior idea of what strategic and tactical decisions will be the right ones to meet the goal. Therefore, at the end of the quarter there will be no surprises if the goals are not met or are exceeded. The manager will have known long in advance the progress made toward the goals.

As we discussed in the introduction, by recognizing that there is always warning and therefore monitoring progress on a daily basis, managers can turn what would have been surprises into a whole new world of opportunity.

Real-Time Opportunity Detection

Predicting the present on its own actually accomplishes very little. Although it may stop an event from being a surprise, that is not enough to ensure business success. If a manager knows that cost of sales is running under target, which would enable a price cut to gain market share without affecting profitability, but does nothing, the opportunity is still missed, the damage is still done. True benefit comes only when the knowledge generated by predicting the present is used to see opportunities and act to change outcomes—what we call *real-time opportunity detection*.

On March 20, 1980, scientists studying seismographs in the Cascade Range in the U.S. Northwest began detecting minor earthquake activity originating around the area of Mount Saint Helens in Washington State. Once the seismic activity was determined to originate from the mountain itself, more specific measurements were taken by seismic equipment right at the site of the volcanic mountain. Seven days later scientists began noticing steam venting from the previously dormant volcano. Shortly after that, scientists reported that a portion of the mountain was "swelling." These signs led scientists to conclude that an eruption of Mount Saint Helens was imminent.

When it became clear that the activity was slowly increasing in frequency and intensity, local government officials heeded the warning signs and issued orders to evacuate. They also prohibited recreational activity near the mountain. Finally, nearly two months after the first seismic readings were detected in the region, Mount Saint Helens erupted. The final toll was more than $3 billion in damage, thousands of animals killed, and millions of trees destroyed, but because of the evacuation orders, only sixty-two people (mostly those who refused to evacuate, although a few were scientists in the process of monitoring the mountain) lost their lives.[2]

There are three main differences between the Galveston hurricane and the Mount Saint Helens eruption. First, of course, is that while there was massive devastation in both natural disasters, thousands fewer people died at Mount Saint Helens. Second, seismologists and volcanologists were predicting the present with real-time information about underground earthquakes, magma flows, ground temperatures, and other measurements to understand the likelihood of a major eruption. Finally, at Mount Saint Helens, because decision makers were predicting the present, they had the opportunity to make decisions that would save lives.

In a world where they are predicting the present, sales executives can see revenue the moment revenue is recognized and can therefore detect opportunities to add incentives or take other actions to boost revenue. Managers are able to see daily profit-and-loss statements, with comparisons to similar periods in the past, and can therefore detect opportunities to invest or cut costs to keep the figures on target. Other executives are able to assess the output of employees in real time and detect opportunities to change the allocation of resources to meet goals. At every moment where predicting the present happens, early warnings can be seen and real-time opportunity detection becomes possible. In the hands of the capable manager, current information about the state of the business always shows opportunities to improve good results or, at a minimum, to act to mitigate the impact of poor results.

In summary:

1. If you acquire the ability to capture, receive, monitor, and analyze information about certain events when those events occur, you can predict the present.

2. If you predict the present and identify the always-present early warnings of difficulties or successes, you will have identified an opportunity for better performance.

3. If you take effective action based on these opportunities, you will be engaged in real-time opportunity detection.

This discussion, of course, begs the question of how to get started in predicting the present and real-time opportunity detection. Before answering that question, we need to look more closely at how the business world functions today and delve more deeply into the mechanics of events, surprises, impacts, and responses.

> **Real-Time Enterprise:** We will go into much more detail regarding Real-Time Enterprises later in the book, but since there is so much hype around the term *Real-Time Enterprise*, it may be helpful to distinguish between real-time opportunity detection and Real-Time Enterprise at this point. A Real-Time Enterprise (RTE) engages in real-time opportunity detection in all its critical business processes by monitoring, capturing, analyzing, and reporting all the events that are critical to the success of the company the moment the events occur. Additionally, an RTE further improves its performance by redesigning all processes needed to respond more efficiently and effectively when required.

A Port to Seek

In the quotation that began this chapter, Henry Adams was comparing ship captains to U.S. presidents. The metaphor applies equally well to successful corporate managers, executives, and officers. Indeed, the similarity between guiding a ship and guiding a business is strong; both require goals and information about the progress toward the goals. And for much of history, ship captains were business managers (many continue to be today) responsible for the return on investment on the voyages they commanded.

One such captain set sail from Sweden in the early spring of 1743 at the direction of the Swedish East India Company on the company's flagship vessel, the Götheborg, en route to Canton, China. The Götheborg had already made two very successful, very profitable voyages to China. This trip, however, was to be different. In September of 1745, more than two years after leaving Sweden, the captain and his ship were finally returning, the cargo hold full to the brim with tea, spices, silks, and porcelain. According to some eyewitness reports, just before entering the harbor, someone (perhaps a representative of the Swedish

East India Company) boarded the ship and informed the captain that the market for the goods he was carrying had collapsed since his departure and that his cargo would not cover the cost of the voyage. Shortly thereafter, the Götheborg, piloted by lifelong sailors from the area, struck a large submerged rock that had been charted for more than two hundred years and that most of the sailors on board must have known about. The ship rapidly sank and the cargo was lost—but miraculously every single person on board managed to escape. The Swedish East India Company and the captain were able to collect a sizeable insurance settlement as a result of the "accident." For all but the last twelve hours of his journey, the captain of the Götheborg had been operating with two-year-old information on the market for spices and porcelain. Based on one piece of information delivered in real time, the captain was able to seek a different "port" with dramatic albeit illegal impact on the return on investment of his voyage.[3]

It is frightening to note how little progress has been made in the last two hundred fifty years in getting better information to managers responsible for steering their initiatives into the right port. Although we infrequently see managers relying on market information that is two years old, in general we think nothing of strategic planning and tactical maneuvering based on last year's market share numbers. Managers are uniformly in the same position as the captain of the Götheborg: steering into port hoping that the market has not changed since the last measurement was taken.

In the introduction, we saw that there is always warning and that disaster can result if individuals are left to make decisions with outdated information that obscured the warning. In each of the cases—Three Mile Island, the Space Shuttle *Challenger*, and September 11—the crucial decision makers were without current information on the situation in which they were making their decisions. In the case of the *Challenger*, the launch decision was made by individuals who believed that the ambient temperatures were in a safe range. At Three Mile Island, the technicians were using training and information that had not been updated with the proper instructions to guard against such accidents. Leading up to September 11, immigration officials were using outdated lists of possible terrorists in granting student visas, certain FBI agents were evaluating activities of foreign students at flight schools with no knowledge of plans to use airplanes as weapons, and the individuals on the first three planes were playing by the now discarded rules of the hostage model of airline hijacking. The heroes of Flight 93, who knew via cell phone conversations with loved ones that this was no "typical" hijacking, show us what happens when individuals have the most current information. They make different and better decisions.

The typical manager is in a similar position to that of the unfortunate people in these examples; she is making critical business decisions in a near-total absence of information about her situation at the moment the decision is made. Captains of ships today have, through the wonders of modern navigation equipment, up-to-the-second information on location, speed, direction, current, and so on. Using the information they can accurately determine the right changes to make to get them safely to the port they seek. Managers today must set out toward their goals with virtually *no* constantly updated information on their progress or about the surrounding conditions. They cannot predict the present because they have no information about the present.

Value of Real-Time Information

Thus far we have used fairly broad examples to illustrate the value of real-time information, predicting the present, and real-time opportunity detection. It's time to be a little more specific. Why is real-time opportunity detection valuable to the manager? Why does predicting the present lead to better decisions? The answer is that real-time information is valuable because it gives the manager the most possible response options.

As illustrated in figure 1-1, the number of possible responses to an event, depicted by the area of the triangle in the diagram, is directly related to the amount of time (shown on the x axis) before the impact of an event is felt. Put another way, as time

FIGURE 1-1

As time passes after an event, the possible responses to the event narrow, depicted by the area of the triangle.

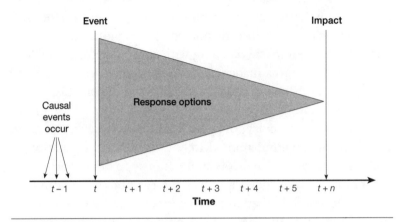

passes after an event occurs, there are fewer and fewer responses that a manager can make to the event before the impact occurs.

Response Options: Response options are actions that may be taken to mitigate the negative impacts or accentuate the positive aspects of an event before the impact of the event is felt. For example, if sales volumes are falling (event), a response option is to increase advertising to improve sales volume before quarterly revenue targets are missed (impact).

Consider, for a moment, driving to work each morning. What would your daily experience be like if you were unable to determine whether the traffic light at each intersection you came to was red or green until you were twenty feet from the intersection? One of two things would happen: (a) you would become used to frantically stomping on the brakes at the last second in an attempt to stop your car before entering an intersection where you didn't have the right-of-way, or (b) you would drive much more slowly as you approached each intersection. Now consider driving to work if you knew the status of traffic lights two miles before you arrived at the intersection and had constantly updated information each time a light changed as you approached. You would have many options available to you—changes in speed, lane, or even route to arrive at each intersection when the light was green. Again, the number and quality of the options available to you to respond to an event (the traffic light turns red) are directly related to the amount of time you have before the impact (colliding with another vehicle) is felt.

Thirty years ago a manager, like our hypothetical driver, had the option of "slowing down"—waiting for information when important strategic decisions were needed. Today's manager doesn't have that luxury; the pace of business has increased and decisions are required immediately even if the information in use is not current. Managers cannot choose to drive their strategies more slowly as they approach "intersections"; they can only learn to accept radical attempts to correct course when information comes in at the last second or not at all. While driving, these radical attempts mean stomping on the brakes; in business this most typically means draconian budget cuts and layoffs when the news is bad or frantic and often poorly planned or executed attempts to capitalize on opportunities when the news is good.

Right Time Versus Real Time

When discussing real-time information there is an unfortunate tendency to mistake real-time information for real-time response. It is critical to understand what parts of the process need to occur in real time and which need only to occur at the "right time." To do so, let's return to our earlier diagram, but now, rather than focusing on response options, let's look at the processes that in the ideal business context happen in the background between an event happening and the impact of the event being felt. Specifically these processes are (1) *monitoring* of information related to the event, (2) *capturing* a change in the information, (3) *analyzing* the information, (4) *reporting* the information, and (5) *responding* to the information.

Modern radar equipment in use on commercial passenger aircraft perhaps illustrates the steps best. The goal of the equipment, known as a traffic collision avoidance system (TCAS), is to prevent planes from colliding with each other in midair. The system was developed after dozens of midair collisions in the 1950s and 1960s as air traffic increased. To accomplish the goal, (1) the system monitors the airspace around the plane using radar; (2) it captures the event of another object coming within a roughly twenty-five-mile radius of the plane; (3) it analyzes the information to determine whether the object is another plane (rather than a bird) and whether the object is on a collision course. If so, (4) the system reports to the pilot this information as well as guidance on how to respond in order to avoid the collision, and (5) the pilot responds. Note that the pilot is not monitoring all information about the surrounding airspace all the time—he has other things to occupy him. But the system is monitoring the information, and the pilot receives real-time information on the airspace when it matters. This is the goal of real-time information—not to turn managers into dashboard watchers but to give them the right information in real time.

Returning to our driving example, let's depict the process as it normally happens for most drivers (figure 1-2). In this case, the event in question is the traffic light at the next intersection turning red. At some point after that, the light comes into view and you begin monitoring it. You capture the information that the light changed to red at some unknown point in the past. Next you analyze the situation and report (to yourself) that you will not have the right-of-way when you reach the intersection. At this point, it is already too late for several response options. You can no longer choose to take an alternate route, for instance. The only available response is to stop the car. All this is undertaken before the occurrence of the quite literal impact that would have taken place had you not stopped. Although the gap between the occurrence of the event and its monitoring, capture, analysis, and reporting created suboptimal results (you still had to stop), disaster was avoided (you didn't have an accident). If this were the way the business world worked most of the time, we wouldn't be in such bad shape.

However, in most business cases, the situation looks more like figure 1-3. The event is not monitored, captured, analyzed, or reported until far too late for effective responses.

FIGURE 1-2

The diagram shows the steps involved in successfully responding to an event: monitoring, capturing, analyzing, reporting, responding, and fine-tuning the response.

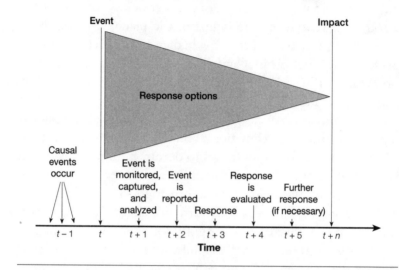

FIGURE 1-3

An event is detected and reported long after it occurs, after many response options are no longer possible.

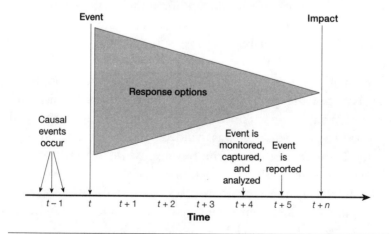

FIGURE 1-4

An event is monitored, captured, analyzed, and reported in real time, allowing the most possible response options. Responses may move earlier or later in the timeline because the manager has the luxury of considering all possible responses and choosing the optimal response and when to invoke it.

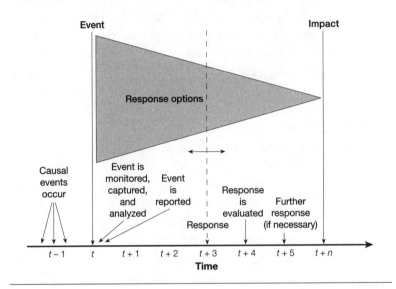

When we discuss real-time information, then, the goal is to move specifically the capture, monitoring, analysis, and reporting steps not just earlier in the process but into real time, as shown in figure 1-4. Moving these steps into real time allows the most possible response options, but just as important, it enables choosing the best response from among them.

It is just as important to note that the response itself does not necessarily move in time, nor does it necessarily move earlier in the process. Of course many times it does, but in some cases it may even come later. In the driving example, consider the situation where you have real-time information reported to you on all the traffic lights on your potential routes. With this information you may determine that although you could change routes to avoid one traffic light that has turned red, the alternate routes will in fact be slower. Therefore a real-time response, without due deliberation, may in fact be more harmful than the original situation. A "right-time" response can be far superior to a real-time response.

Although real-time information on events is always helpful, real-time response is being shown in a number of cases to do more harm than good. Recent studies of certain cancers have shown that early detection (read: monitor, capture, analyze, report) does not lead to higher survival rates. Doctors are concluding that the reason for this lack of improved results is due to an overly aggressive response. Although real-time information on the presence of a tumor allows a wide variety of responses, to date many doctors have been responding with the most aggressive treatments, which may be more harmful to overall health than the tumor.[4] The same is true in business. Think of the manager who changes strategies monthly. Overly aggressive responses to real-time information may yield no better results than those achieved without any real-time information at all.

This is the difference between real time and right time. Monitoring, capture, analysis, and reporting of critical information must move to real time so that predicting the present and real-time opportunity detection can take place. They will determine the "right time" for a response to achieve maximum positive results.

Opportunity Versus Disaster

The main topic of this book is ending business surprises, events that occur with seemingly no warning. Before we proceed, it will be helpful to talk about the different types of events that occur in the business world—*surprises, opportunities,* and *disasters.* As the examples in the introduction showed, the events that truly arrive with no warning are few and far between. For virtually all events, warning is available, although it may not be in the right hands or not in the right hands until it is too late. Let's break the various types of events down into three categories defined by the monitor, capture, analyze, report, and respond steps and look at some examples of each type (figure 1-5).

FIGURE 1-5

The three types of events are differentiated by what steps are accomplished before the impact is felt.

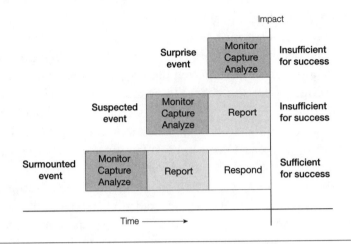

Surprise event: The event is not reported, in some cases because it was not monitored, captured, or analyzed.

The discovery in 1994 that Aldrich Ames, a high-ranking officer of the CIA, had been spying for the KGB and its successors for nine years is a good example of a surprise event. During the period when he was spying, Ames had spent more than three times his total salary. He had also been caught in a variety of acts that were specifically prohibited by the CIA. However, none of the CIA investigators used this information to predict the present and detect the opportunity to stop the spy who eventually caused the deaths of at least nine CIA informants.[5]

In this case, as in many other surprise events, the information was readily available but no one was monitoring it, much less reporting it. The Three Mile Island, *Challenger,* and September 11 examples we looked at in the introduction would also fall into this category.

ending business surprises

> **Suspected event:** The event is monitored, captured, ana-
> lyzed, and reported but too late for effective action.

The Galveston hurricane and the Internet investment bubble
discussed at the beginning of the introduction were suspected
events. The famous surprise sinking of the *Titanic* is another example. Just before the *Titanic* struck the iceberg that ripped it
open, the lookout on duty spotted the berg. He radioed the news
to the bridge where the officer in charge ordered the engines
stopped and reversed and the ship turned hard to starboard. As
we all know, however, the ship could not turn in time. The
warning was received too late and the *Titanic* struck the iceberg.

A more timely example of this type of event occurred in June
2000: the Hayman forest fire in the Pike–San Isabel National
Forest, approximately thirty miles southwest of Denver, Colorado. In the days leading up to the fire, the temperature in the
Pike National Forest area had risen above ninety degrees, wind
gusts had increased, and the moisture level of the trees, leaves,
and other "ground fuel" had become approximately 30 percent
lower than kiln-dried lumber used for construction.[6] In view of
these fire hazard conditions, the forest service issued a ban on
the use of fire throughout the entire area. On June 8, Terry Barton, a forest service employee, while on patrol to enforce the
fire ban, decided to use a campfire ring to burn some personal
letters. After the letters had been consumed, she buried the fire.
When she thought the fire had been completely extinguished
she left the site. However, as she was departing from the area,
she noticed that the fire was in fact still burning and had escaped
the confines of the campfire ring. After the failure of a desperate
attempt to once again put out the fire on her own, Barton called
in to report the rapidly growing conflagration. By the time a fire
engine arrived at the site, however, the fire was already out of
control.[7] When the inferno was finally contained on July 2, Colorado's largest fire in history had claimed more than 137,000
acres, 133 homes, a commercial building, and 466 outbuild-
ings.[8] Barton's desire to conceal the cause of the fire led to a significant delay in reporting that in turn prevented the available

response options from being effective. Remarkably, this kind of behavior is one of the most frequent causes of suspected events. Fearing discovery of poor results, individuals withhold information and do not report bad news to relevant parties until it is too late to react.

Surmounted event: The event is reported in time and effective action is taken.

The eruption of Mount Saint Helens is an example of a surmounted event. Scientists detected the warning signs of an imminent eruption and state officials took effective action to ensure that the smallest possible number of people was in harm's way.

Although it's impossible to say whether the major events of September 11 constituted a surprise event, other events that day were most definitely surmounted events. eBay, one of the largest e-commerce sites in the world, realized less than an hour after the collapse of the first tower of the World Trade Center that someone had put pieces of rubble up for auction on their site. By predicting the present, the specifics of which we'll discuss in much more detail in chapter 5, executives at eBay were able to respond effectively to the callous listings. eBay's reputation and public standing undoubtedly were saved from significant damage by seeing opportunity in real time and responding appropriately.

Trying to classify an event into one of the three types can be confusing. The confusion is due to the fact that the "correct" category for an event depends entirely on the point of reference. A quick example: For the millions of people who replaced the tires on their Ford Explorers after the Consumer Product Safety Commission, Ford, and Firestone recalled certain SUV tires because of a risk of catastrophic tire failure leading to vehicle rollovers, the event (the discovery of systemic separation of tire tread) was a surmounted event. Warning signs of tire failure were detected and appropriate action was taken. However, for

---

BEYOND THE SURMOUNTED EVENT

For simplicity's sake, the preceding descriptions end with surmounted events where an effective response is possible. However, we recognize that simply responding is not the only issue. Optimal results do not always materialize as a result of an initial response. Ideally, a response is undertaken far enough in advance of the impact to allow time for evaluating the efficacy of the response (based on capturing, analyzing, and reporting the results) and for refining the response where warranted.

Of course, there is nothing new in evaluating the efficacy of a response to determine whether refinements to the initial response are in order. But in the context of real-time opportunity detection, employees, managers, and executives must find the time to conduct such evaluations in order to reach appropriately refined responses. Making time for response evaluation places a greater degree of pressure on managers to shorten the time required to report and respond to events.

---

the families who suffered the loss of a loved one due to the tire failures, the event was a suspected event: It was discovered too late for effective action; the damage had already been done.

The difference between an event we call an opportunity and one we call a disaster most often depends on which of the categories the event falls into. Even an event like the eruption of Mount Saint Helens, despite the devastation to the surrounding environment, can be seen as an opportunity, an opportunity for those who were evacuated out of danger to continue their lives. And the opportunity arose because what could have been a surprise event or suspected event was instead a surmounted event, thanks to the volcanologists and seismologists who predicted the present and to the relevant authorities who performed real-time opportunity detection.

Ending business surprises doesn't require psychics or tea leaves. In fact, no knowledge of the future is required. It simply requires that managers receive a heads-up about the present—a few vital elements of data about what is happening right now in their business. Using this information, a manager can successfully understand the big picture at any given moment—what we have called predicting the present. Using this real-time understanding of what is happening in his business, any manager has the chance to take action to prevent surprises and turn them into opportunities.

This conversion of surprises and disasters into opportunities is where we now turn our attention. In chapter 2, we'll discuss the methodology for gathering and monitoring the information that will help you turn surprise and suspected events—disasters—into surmounted events—opportunities.

2

identifying and justifying the right real-time information

Forewarned, forearmed; to be prepared is half the victory.
—Don Quixote

A<small>T THE END OF</small> World War II, many people in the United States felt absolutely confident that they lived in the most powerful country on earth. Their confidence was shattered just four years later when, on August 29, 1949, the Soviet Union detonated its first nuclear device. American scientists and officials within the U.S. intelligence community had woefully underestimated how close the Soviets were to developing and deploying their own atomic bomb. Their shock was amplified when sources revealed the rapid rate at which the Soviet Union was also building long-range bombers. These two pieces of information led to the inescapable conclusion that the continental United States was vulnerable to nuclear attack by the Soviet Union.

In response to the new threat, senior military planners convened a group of elite scientists in the summer of 1952 to determine how best to defend the United States from this new and
frightening possibility. The group soon concluded that the most
likely direction of attack would be over the North Pole because
this was the shortest distance between Soviet air bases and major
U.S. population centers. Further, they determined that the only
way to prevent a nuclear attack coming over the pole was to deploy a line of radar installations to comprehensively cover every
single mile of territory between the two countries. The radar
line also had to communicate the presence of any aircraft instantly to the central air defense command (known then as
CONAD, now as NORAD) to allow an immediate response.

FIGURE 2-1

**The DEW Line was installed to protect the United States
from airborne nuclear attack by the Soviet Union.**

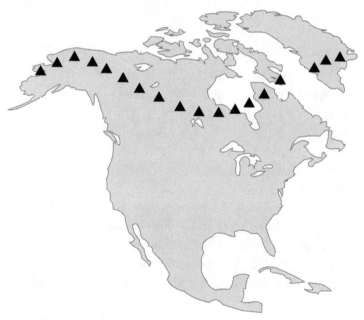

Source: Gartner, Inc., based on NORAD data.

By 1954, the Distant Early Warning (DEW) Line, one of the greatest yet largely unknown feats of modern engineering, had been completed (figure 2-1). The DEW Line provided real-time comprehensive radar coverage across 3,000 miles of tundra from Point Barrow, Alaska, to the eastern edge of Canada. At the time of its completion, the DEW Line would have warned of a Soviet attack four to six hours in advance of the appearance of enemy bombers over populated areas of the United States, enough time to attempt to intercept the attack before it reached its target and the irrevocable consequences of atomic weapons were unleashed.[1]

As critical as the DEW Line was to ensuring the nation's safety—to ensuring that we never woke up to the "surprise" of a Soviet nuclear attack (or failed to wake up at all)—at the time of its completion there were still large holes in the nation's ability to monitor the approach of aircraft on other borders. There was no immediate effort to build a similar line along the Mexican border, for instance.

The United States did not have comprehensive radar coverage of *all* the nation's borders; it had coverage of just the most important ones. In a similar manner, the manager looking to guide her business to the successful attainment of goals needs real-time information about *some* but not *all* aspects of operations.

Just Because You Can Doesn't Mean You Should

Clearly, the U.S. military could have built a radar perimeter around the entire country—or the entire continent, for that matter. It is obvious why no such effort was undertaken: There were much better ways to spend a limited amount of resources for defending the nation than protecting against the unlikely possibility of an aerial attack from the south. The NORAD personnel responsible for monitoring the real-time information coming from the DEW Line were watching roughly only 35 percent of the total border areas of the United States; the percentage would be much smaller if you considered all the potential U.S. targets not located in the continental United States (military bases in Western Europe, Japan, and the Korean peninsula, for instance).

A manager could attempt to monitor every operational variable in real time, but there are far better ways to utilize limited resources, even though rapid advances in technologies like radio frequency identification, portals, wireless communications, and Web services are dramatically driving down costs. Over time, the resources that are limited will become less financial and technological and more time-based—managers will not have the time to track all the information they can affordably monitor. Just as in the defense of the United States, only a small percentage, perhaps 5 percent, of the potential operational data is required to predict the present and begin real-time opportunity detection.

Nineteenth-century department store magnate John Wanamaker is reputed to have commented, "Half my advertising is wasted. I just don't know which half." Similarly, the difficult part of choosing real-time information candidates is determining which 5 percent to monitor.

Identification and Justification

Given that every attempt to monitor any piece of information in real time costs resources—whether information technology resources or just the time taken for monitoring—the manager must identify what information should be monitored in real time and whether the effort required to obtain and monitor the information in real time is justified. Let's call the process Identification and Justification.

What information should be monitored depends, of course, entirely on who the individual employee, supervisor, manager, or executive is. Consider again a ship captain, this time on a modern vessel. Clearly, given the state of technology today and easily available tools, the captain could monitor the moment-to-moment status of a vast array of conditions or events affecting the ship, including the temperature of the refrigeration unit and the number of fish in the immediate vicinity. Would this information qualify as worthy of being monitored and worth the expense of installing the necessary sensors? If the ship in question is an oil tanker, the answer, of course, would be "No." If, however, the ship is catching tuna for the sushi markets in Tokyo, the answer would be a definitive "YES!"

Unfortunately, the right answers to the question of what information to monitor and whether it is worth the effort to begin monitoring, capturing, and reporting it is not so obvious for most managers. Their responsibilities are many and varied and depend on a wide variety of processes and influences both internal and external to their organization. Consider a product manager for a consumer packaged goods company, Consumer Products, Inc., with specific revenue and profitability targets for the year. Reaching the targets depends on many, many factors: the price of the product, competitive products, competitive pricing, sales force attention, shelf space in major retail outlets, the state of the economy, consumer spending, quality, availability, materials costs, advertising effectiveness—the list could go on and on. When confronted with a long list of influences on goals, anyone would be tempted to throw up their hands and exclaim, "That's too many things to monitor in real time!" Of course that's true. But recall that the goal is to predict the present, and predicting the present does not require monitoring every piece of operational data, just the critical ones.

How does the manager determine which of the wide variety of influences on reaching her goals is necessary for predicting the present and therefore worthy of being monitored, captured, and reported in real time? By filtering all the possible information candidates through the Identification and Justification Models to determine which are worth monitoring in real time (figure 2-2).

Identification Model

A friend of mine lived in Marin County, California, during one of the awful wildfire seasons there. At one point, the police came down her street and announced that everyone had to leave their homes within thirty minutes; residents who did not would be forcibly removed. "At that moment, forced to choose what

FIGURE 2-2

The Identification and Justification Models help reduce the many candidates for real-time monitoring to the few that are worth it.

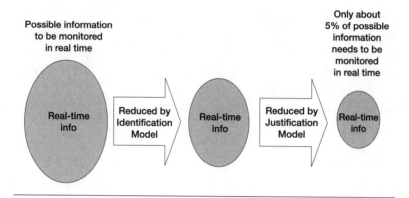

Possible information to be monitored in real time

Only about 5% of possible information needs to be monitored in real time

Real-time info → Reduced by Identification Model → Real-time info → Reduced by Justification Model → Real-time info

few things to rescue from the house, it suddenly became very clear what my priorities were, what things we had accumulated were worth saving," she told me. Each manager considering candidates for predicting the present needs to put himself through a similar "trial by fire" to determine priorities.

Step 1 of the Identification Model, List Goals (figure 2-3), requires determining the list of all of the goals for the quarter, year, planning period—whatever is relevant in the individual case—and determining the metrics by which achievement of the goals will be measured. Often the metrics are stated explicitly in the goals ("Achieve 22 percent market share," "Generate $20 million in revenue and $3 million in profit"). If not, the metrics need to be clarified, for they are the actual information to potentially be tracked in real time. In cases where the metrics are not immediately apparent, those chosen must be valid (they must correspond to the goals being measured) and reliable (they can be accurately and objectively measured over time without undue error).[2]

In Step 2 of the model, Prioritize, look at the list of goals and ask yourself, "If I could reach only a few of these goals, which ones would be most likely to ensure corporate and per-

FIGURE 2-3

In the Identification Model, business goals and causal events are identified, prioritized, and evaluated.

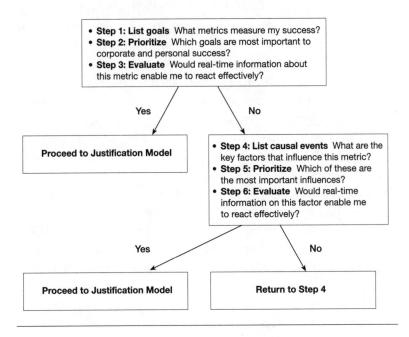

sonal success?" Put another way, if a fire was threatening to destroy your office and all records of what you accomplished in the last year, what pieces of evidence would you save? This process of clearly defining goals, the metrics by which they are measured, and narrowing the goals down to the most important—determining the priority—is essential in determining what information should be considered for predicting the present.

Stories are told of the "seeker" asking the "guru," "What is the secret of life?" The response is always something like, "It's just one thing, but you have to figure out what the one thing is for yourself." If the secret to achieving a happy and meaningful life were truly this simple, we would all probably be much happier. If managers could identify just one thing to measure their success by, certainly their jobs would be easier. Most managers will not be able to narrow their various goals down to just "one thing." However, it is crucial to eliminate every item that is not absolutely critical for success before taking the next step. That said, many managers are able to narrow the list to only two, three, or four items instead of just one. Our research findings constantly reinforce the conclusion that most employees, managers, and executives need only very few items monitored, captured, and analyzed in real time. While any number of information candidates can be run through the next steps of the process, this should not be an excuse for not applying the utmost rigor in determining the smallest number of critical areas possible.

For managers with a profit-and-loss (P&L) statement, narrowing the list is relatively easy. A quick comparison of the relative sizes of various figures on the revenue and expense sides of the income statement helps identify some of the most important items to consider capturing and monitoring in real time. Another guide is to focus on variable costs, not fixed costs. Neither of these guidelines is a hard and fast rule, however. Neither the largest items nor the variable costs are always the most important items to consider monitoring. Both managers with P&Ls and those without need to consider the many nonfinancial metrics that may be crucial to their success; for example, customer satisfaction, employee retention, or brand loyalty. Certainly it has been proven that management focus on financial metrics alone can lead to devastating results—cutting costs to satisfy a single-minded focus on profits has put many companies in a downward spiral as their ability to produce the products or provide the level of service that attracts customers is diminished. In many cases managers can look to the operations management framework, such as Balanced Scorecard, activity-based costing, or the European Foundation for Quality Management, in use in their business for guidance in determining the highest-priority goals, particularly the nonfinancial ones.

Let's return to our product manager at Consumer Products, Inc. After evaluating her P&L and nonfinancial high-priority metrics and running herself through the imaginary "trial by fire," she determines that her personal success depends on profitability but that corporate success depends more on the attainment of revenue and customer satisfaction targets. Therefore, she decides to take the next step with revenue, customer satis-

IDENTIFICATION MODEL AND THE BALANCED SCORECARD

The Balanced Scorecard, an idea originally introduced in a *Harvard Business Review* article in 1992, helps company employees build a portfolio of metrics that combine "measures of past performance with measures of the drivers of future performance."[3] In their methodology, authors David P. Norton and Robert K. Kaplan declare four major categories that warrant tracking by clear performance measures: (1) financial performance, (2) customers, (3) internal business processes, and (4) learning and growth. Examples of Balanced Scorecard performance metrics are shown in table 2-1.

The authors stress that while financial metrics reflect performance in the past, customer, internal business process, and learning and growth metrics can be leading indicators of future results. Therefore, for companies who are using the Balanced Scorecard or any other operational performance management system that specifies metrics the organization believes to be leading indicators, the metrics should be carefully considered as options in Steps 1 and 2 of the Identification Model.

TABLE 2-1

Sample Balanced Scorecard Metrics

Area	Metrics
Financial	Sales growth rates, market share for regions[a]
Customer	Speedy service, friendly employees[b]
Internal business processes	Number of times new products had to be modified[c]
Learning and growth	Number of employees being retrained[d]

a. Robert K. Kaplan and David P. Norton, *The Balanced Scorecard: Translating Strategy into Action* (Boston: Harvard Business School Press, 1996), 51.
b. Ibid., 83.
c. Ibid., 102.
d. Ibid., 134.

faction, and profitability from the product as possible metrics for monitoring in real time.

That next step, Step 3, Evaluate, is to ask of each of the candidates: "Would real-time information on this metric enable me to react effectively?" In chapter 1, using the graphic shown

ending business surprises

again in figure 2-4, we discussed how the number of possible responses to change outcomes diminishes as the amount of time
since the event increases and the amount of time before the impact decreases. In the driving example in chapter 1, we assumed
that there was enough of a gap in time, or event–impact lag, between the event (the light changing) and the impact (a collision
with another vehicle) to allow for an appropriate response
(using the brakes to stop the car).

> **Event–Impact Lag:** An event–impact lag is the amount of
> time separating an event and its impact. The event–impact
> lag can be infinitesimal—for example, the amount of time
> between an Olympic marksman pulling the trigger on his
> rifle (the event) and the bullet hitting the target (the im-
> pact)—or very large—the amount of time between the use
> of lead paint in a house (event) and brain damage in a tod-
> dler (impact) years later .

In the business world, however, this is clearly not always the
case. At this stage of determining what information to monitor

FIGURE 2-4

**In Step 3 of the Identification Model, the possibility of
responses within the confines of the event–impact lag is
evaluated.**

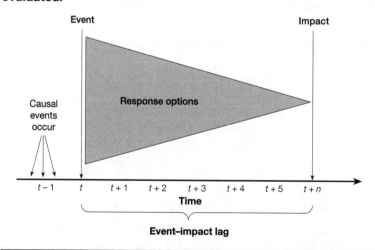

in real time, the manager needs to closely assess the relationship between the event–impact lag and the response options available. In some cases the lag between event and impact is several months, in other cases minutes or even seconds. Obviously, the shorter the lag the more quickly a response is required. For present purposes the issue to consider is how much time the available responses take in relation to the event–impact lag. If the possible responses can be undertaken in the time allowed (within the event–impact lag), then this metric is a good candidate for predicting the present (it passes the Identification Model). At this point, the manager should move on to considering whether the effort to monitor this information in real time is justified (see the next section, Justification Model). If, however, possible response options take too long (longer than the event–impact lag), then the answer is "No" and further steps are necessary.

For a bit more clarity on this point, let's return to the captain on the sushi boat. Imagine that the captain was considering monitoring the temperature of the refrigeration unit in real time. In this case the captain considers the information to be monitored and the event to be captured, analyzed, and reported—the temperature in the refrigeration unit rising above or falling below certain threshold levels—and the impact of that event—the spoiling of the tuna. The lag between the temperature rising above, say, 70 degrees Fahrenheit and the tuna spoiling is perhaps twelve hours. Now the captain needs to consider possible responses. If there is a backup refrigeration unit on board that takes thirty minutes to start up, then the response option fits well within the event–impact lag and the captain should begin evaluating whether the effort to obtain real-time information on the refrigeration unit is justified. However, if there is no backup refrigeration unit on board and the only possible response option is a trip back to port that requires more than twelve hours, then the response option does not fit within the event–impact lag; the captain should then move on to the next step in the Identification Model.

The next necessary steps begin with an analysis of the causes of the event originally considered. Every event is part of a chain of causes and impacts, as shown in figure 2-5.

IT'S ALL RELATIVE

It may be hard at times to determine what is an event and what is an impact. In the last chapter we noted that the difference between a surprise, suspected, or surmounted event can depend solely on who is looking at the situation; the same is true in determining what constitutes an event, a cause, or an impact. In a simple chain of advertising leads to sales leads to profits leads to share price growth, three different managers may have three different perspectives on which of these is an impact, an event, or a causal event. To the marketing manager, the event is advertising and sales is the impact; to the financial analyst, advertising is the causal event, sales is the event, and profits is the impact. To the CEO, profit is the event and share price growth is the impact. In the end, applying these labels is a subjective choice of each manager that matters very little—the important thing is to use the terminology consistently.

In general, Step 1, List Goals, and Step 2, Prioritize, identify events that are near the end of the chain of causes and impacts that affect the manager. If it is determined that the response options for the event in question do not fit in the event–impact lag, in Step 4, List Causal Events, the manager must determine the causes of the event originally considered. The sushi boat captain who determines that the response option of returning to

FIGURE 2-5

Each event has an impact, which in turn causes other impacts; whether an occurrence is an event or an impact depends on your perspective.

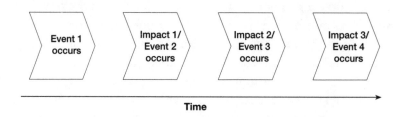

port does not fit within the time between the rise of temperatures in the refrigeration unit and the spoiling of the fish would then list the possible causes of the failure of the refrigeration unit. The causes might include mechanical failure, a fall in refrigerant levels, or a loss of power on the boat.

As this example illustrates, the chains of causes and impacts are generally more complex than figure 2-5 shows. In most cases, an event-impact chain would be more realistically presented as shown in figure 2-6, with perhaps many more events linked as causes in the chain. In Step 5, Prioritize, the manager must take all the relevant causal events and prioritize them, as was done with goals at the beginning of the process, determining the most significant or most likely cause. Again, the desired outcome is to choose only the causes that are crucial—if not one, then the fewest number possible. In Step 6, Evaluate, the manager should then ask of these causes/events the same question considered before: Would real-time information about this cause enable me to respond effectively?

FIGURE 2-6

Rarely is there only one cause of an impact. Usually there are several causal events.

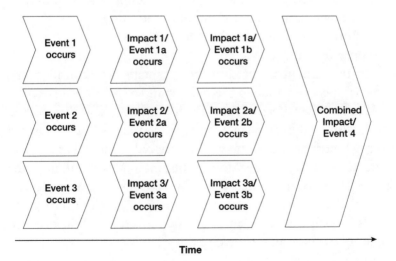

FIGURE 2-7

By identifying earlier events in the chain of events and impacts, a manager can expand the event-impact lag and expand response options.

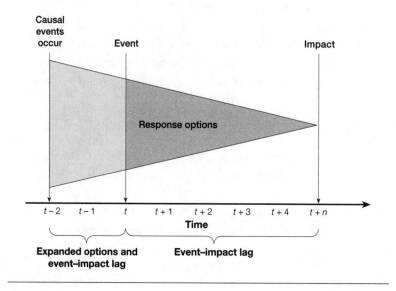

Now the event–impact lag diagram will look like figure 2-7. Seen from the perspective of the causal event, the event originally considered is now the first of several impacts. By monitoring an event earlier in the chain of events and impacts, there is now both more time available for responses and more possible response options.

In this instance, our sushi boat captain now considers the time lag between a fall in the refrigerant levels below an acceptable range, the failure of the refrigerant system, and the spoiling of the fish. If this time lag exceeds the amount of time required to reach port and have the system serviced, he now has a candidate to evaluate against the Justification Model. If not, the process is repeated once again by returning to Step 4, List Causal Events, with the causes of the falling of the refrigerant levels investigated until an event is discovered with a sufficient time lag to allow an effective response.

Now let's run through the whole process with the product manager at Consumer Products, Inc. Recall that she has determined that revenue, customer satisfaction, and profitability are the three most important goals to consider. First she considers whether real-time information on revenue to date will allow a response that falls within the lag time between the event (revenue not tracking on required path) and the impact (revenue target is missed). If the product sells at a steady and constant rate where no time period disproportionately accounts for total sales—for instance, toothpaste—then the answer is most likely to be "Yes." Real-time information on sales falling out of the expected path would enable a variety of options—discounts, rebates, advertising, sales force incentives—that might bring sales back to the levels required for success. However, if the product sells in irregular patterns—for example, most of the sales of snow blowers happen in a short period in December and January each year—real-time information on revenue may not allow enough time for a response. (For the sake of argument, imagine that three weeks are required for the issuing of rebates and increased advertising to have an impact in the market.) In that case, the product manager may determine that the two most important causal events are shelf space at home improvement warehouses and inventory levels (for replenishing sold stock). Next she evaluates again what response options are possible within the event–impact lag. Here she determines that real-time information on shelf space will enable effective responses to increase shelf space, lessening the impact of falling sales, but inventory levels cannot be increased fast enough even with real-time information. She therefore follows the trail of causes and determines that parts stocks (for example, engines and exhaust assemblies) and available manufacturing capacity are the major influences on inventory. Finally, the lag between monitoring real-time information on parts stocks and manufacturing capacity and missing revenue targets is sufficient to allow for effective response options to influence sales.

Let's pause briefly to consider how the event–impact lag can vary. If the revenue target is a quarterly one, the event–impact lag shortens as the end of the quarter approaches. Therefore the options available for responding to a revenue shortfall decrease with each passing day. Good management dictates aiming high enough above targets to compensate for the loss of options as the target approaches. Just as the ship captain strives to reach his destination slightly early and begins taking course and speed measurements more often as the ship approaches port, the manager may need to narrow the thresholds that spur a reaction as the end of the quarter approaches and ensure that there is sufficient overachievement to compensate for any variances that occur too late for reaction even with real-time information. The key here is not to judge real-time information candidates by the smallest potential event–impact lag (one day before the end of the quarter) but by the normal event–impact lag (an average of forty-five days before the end of the quarter).

After following a similar process for profitability and customer satisfaction, the product manager determines that these measures are less volatile and therefore that measuring them in real time will allow adequate response times. The good news is that the product manager now has several good candidates for information to be captured, monitored, and reported in real time, which will allow predicting the present and real-time opportunity detection: parts stocks, manufacturing capacity, retail shelf space, profitability, and customer satisfaction. The bad news is that she is only halfway through the process.

Justification Model

As the product manager at Consumer Products, Inc., did, a manager using the Identification Model is likely to arrive at several candidates for real-time capture, monitoring, and reporting. Given that almost certainly all the candidates will not be immediately available, the manager must prioritize the candidates to determine which to pursue first. Additionally, as we all learned in basic economics classes, we live in a world of finite resources, and as many economist pundits like to repeat, "There is no such thing as a free lunch." Finite resources will have to be expended to capture, monitor, and report real-time information. In the Identification Model, we were evaluating what pieces of information may be worth the manager's time to monitor. Bringing about real-time monitoring, capture, analysis, and reporting will require more than just the manager's time, however. It will almost certainly require resources under the control of other managers, and therefore a justification for the allocation of the resources will be required.

Once candidate(s) for real-time monitoring and reporting have been identified using the Identification Model, they must be evaluated against the Justification Model. When considering the DEW Line, it is somewhat intuitively obvious that although protecting the continental United States from aerial attack was a priority, it was not worth the time, expense, and effort to build a DEW Line along the Mexican border.

Determining which candidates generated by the Identification Model are most important (highest priority) and which are worth the effort required to obtain them (justification for resources) forces managers to use more than just intuition. Each candidate generated by the Identification Model must pass through a further series of tests—the Justification Model (figure 2-8).

The Justification Model acts like a funnel, further narrowing down candidates from the Identification Model. Each step is a more stringent test that fewer candidates pass:

- *Question 1:* Does the goal the information will help you to achieve support the corporate vision and mission?

- *Question 2:* Does the goal align with current corporate priorities?

- *Question 3:* Is the information material to the goal, *or* would this information alone propel you to take action?

- *Question 4:* What is the corporate impact of achieving (or not achieving) the goal?

Corporate Vision and Mission

Alignment is one of the buzzwords of our age; the number of consulting studies and business books that discuss the impor-

FIGURE 2-8

In the Justification Model, candidates for monitoring in real time are evaluated against corporate goals and materiality.

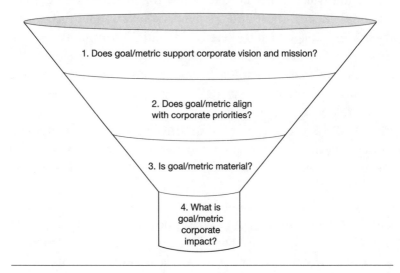

1. Does goal/metric support corporate vision and mission?

2. Does goal/metric align with corporate priorities?

3. Is goal/metric material?

4. What is goal/metric corporate impact?

tance of properly aligning everything from pay scales to strategic plans is mind-numbing. Unfortunately, when a business concept is overused, we tend to lose sight of the inherent value—and there is much inherent value in ensuring that daily tasks are aligned with long-term goals. The same is true for real-time information candidates. If the goals the information supports are not aligned with the overall corporate goals, it is extremely unlikely that (a) the necessary resources to begin capturing and reporting the information will be made available or (b) it is worth the manager's time to monitor the information.

Much has been written about the importance of clear corporate vision and mission statements in books like *Built to Last* by Jim Collins and Jerry Porras (New York: HarperBusiness, 1994). Mission statements are the foundation for aligning the efforts of all the individuals across the company and for determining priorities. It may seem that it would go without saying that the goals of the manager must support corporate vision and mission, but this seemingly obvious step has been missed too many times for us to ignore.

Current Corporate Priorities

Clearly, even with the best-written vision and mission statements, there are many possible ways to support a corporate vision and mission. How does one determine what the current corporate priorities for achieving the mission and vision are so that alignment can be evaluated? There are several places to look:

Corporate Strategic Business Plan

Basic texts and guides to creating a strategic business plan generally advise the inclusion in a written plan of the following elements:

- Vision
- Mission
- Values
- Objectives
- Strategies
- Goals
- Programs

Once management has established the *vision* (a view of the market and other conditions the business will operate within in the future) and finalized the *mission* (the reason the company exists), the *values* section describes how business activities will be conducted.

The most important of the elements to consider when determining priorities are the last four:

- *Objectives* are set to establish broad expectations for employees and shareholders and to provide an outline of the general conditions, situations, or state planners hope to achieve as a result of the execution of the plan.

- *Strategies* establish the basic parameters of how the desired results will be reached.

- *Goals* provide the answer to the question "What specifically are we expected to accomplish?" and specify the time by which the accomplishments are to be attained.

- *Programs* are the specific sets of activities that will be utilized to achieve the objectives, strategies, and goals.

The objectives, strategies, and goals should clearly answer questions about priorities, such as revenue growth versus profitability, market share goals, cost savings, return on assets, and so on.

Cheat Sheets

Often a manager needs to look beyond the corporate strategic business plan because it is outdated or it simply does not exist. Executive presentations to members of the investment community, which I colloquially refer to as "cheat sheets," are particularly useful in this situation. These documents are helpful because they contain the measures by which CEOs and other executives will be evaluated by shareholders and which therefore will most definitely be the priorities of the executives. Two examples of cheat sheets appear in figures 2-9 and 2-10; one is from SBC Communications, Inc., the other from Alcoa, Inc. They show the priorities of the senior executives as these executives articulated them to Wall Street analysts.

Clearly, overall cost discipline is a value and keeping capital expenditures below $8 billion is a priority at SBC. Although Alcoa does not go into such specifics, capital management seems one of the preeminent goals.

Forward-Looking Statements in Public Filings

Another stand-in for a strategic business plan is the forward-looking statements that appear in most SEC filings and primarily describe the expected performance of the company but also expectations of market conditions, including competitor strategies and regulatory actions that may occur in the future. The statements commonly use words like *anticipates, believes, estimates, expects, may, plans, predicts, should,* and so on. They provide insight into the current priorities of a company as well as

FIGURE 2-9

This slide from an SBC investor presentation clearly spells out company goals.

Three Focus Areas

- Cost discipline
  - Companywide initiative to change cost structure
  - 2002 cap ex below $8 billion

- Marketing initiatives
  - New bundling strategies
  - Unified sales and marketing organization

- Leadership to help move industry to stability—with a sustainable investment model, in a rational regulatory and competitive environment

Source: SBC presentation from SBC Communications, Inc., "Three Focus Areas." The slide was available at <http://www.sbc.com/investor_relations/company_reports_and_sec_filings/0,5931,282,00.html> (accessed 5 September 2002). It can now be obtained from SBC's Investor Relations Group.

FIGURE 2-10

This slide from an Alcoa investor presentation also delineates company goals.

Closing the Gap

- Goal remains the same—*top quintile*

- How do we attain?
  - Growth
  - Cost reduction
  - Fixed capital management
  - Working capital management

Source: Data from Alcoa, "Closing the Gap" (paper presented at Second Quarter Analyst Conference, New York, 17 July 2002). The slide is available at <http://www.alcoa.com/global/en/investment/pdfs/2Q02_Analyst_Workshop.pdf> (accessed 4 September 2002). 2000 NYSE data based on 2,862 listed companies.

the aspects of the market and corporate operations that will receive a high level of attention in the months and years ahead.

Once the priorities of the corporation are established through one of these sources, the manager needs to compare them to the goals he or she is trying to achieve through predicting the present. If, for instance, the product manager at Consumer Products, Inc., worked instead for SBC, she would compare the goals she was trying to achieve with the corporate values and priorities enumerated in SBC's cheat sheets. The conclusion would be that while revenue was a goal of hers, cost management was a priority of the company, and therefore she would be unlikely to get the resources necessary to begin capturing shelf space, for instance, in real time. She would be better served by returning to the Identification Model and beginning again with profitability or expenses rather than revenue.

Evaluating individual goals against corporate priorities may lead to conflict when alignment between the individual manager's most important goals and corporate priorities does not exist. In this case, several courses of action are possible, depending on the amount of resources needed to obtain the required information in real time and who has control over the resources. If the information is already readily available, there is no issue. If significant resources are required, the manager (and the overall corporate entity) would be better served by the manager focusing on goals that may be farther down his priority list but that do align with corporate priorities.

Materiality

If the goals supported by the real-time information are aligned with corporate vision, mission, and priorities, then the next test is materiality. The Financial Accounting Standards Board defines information as material when it is "probable that the judgment of a reasonable person relying on the information would have been changed or influenced" if the information had been different.[4]

All candidates for real-time monitoring and reporting must be evaluated for materiality, meaning that a reasonable person (in this case, the manager) would change a decision or a course of action based on the information. Many have heard the famous analogy of chaos theory that Atlantic hurricanes are caused by a butterfly flapping its wings in Beijing. The Identification Model's insistence on considering information for real-time monitoring only when it allows sufficient time for an adequate response tends to lead far back along the cause–impact chain. Materiality acts as a powerful counterbalance against that tendency. If cause–impact chains are followed back as far as the butterfly in Beijing, the materiality of the information may be in question. Even if it were possible to trace the cause of hurricanes back to such a minor disturbance, it is unlikely that the governor of Florida would order evacuations whenever a butterfly grew impatient in China. The governor would seek information much farther along the cause–impact chain for confirmation before acting. One of the reasons, of course, is that the farther you move back in an event–impact chain, the more the direct causality of the event becomes diffused; it can be debated whether the purported cause really is a cause.

After determining that the goals the manager seeks to reach by predicting the present and engaging in real-time opportunity detection align properly with corporate vision, mission, and priorities, the manager needs to ask: "Will this piece of information—this piece of information alone—propel me into action?" This was true of the military planners who built and operated the DEW Line. Seeing any unidentified planes approaching the United States over the pole would have propelled them into action. However, it is far less clear that a similar number of unidentified planes approaching from Mexico would have propelled even a remotely similar reaction (planners would have waited for further confirmation). Therefore, building the DEW Line along the Mexican border would not have passed the materiality test.

You might wonder why the materiality test comes so late in the process of evaluating candidates for transformation into real-time information. Many might consider materiality an appropriate first test of candidates. However, our research found that individuals' perception of the materiality of information

---

COST JUSTIFICATION

Where does the question of cost come in? The answer is not until now. Cost considerations have been deliberately avoided until this point for two reasons: (1) each company has its own methods and processes for computing cost and return, particularly in projects that require IT resources; (2) there is no reason to consider the cost of transforming any information that does not pass all the tests—if the information does not pass the tests, it is not worth monitoring in real time, regardless of cost.

The manager who has followed the models diligently should have all the information needed to enter the cost justification process, whatever it is in his or her organization. There are too many cost justification methodologies to count, but in essence they all balance cost against benefit. Armed with the answers to the questions of the Identification and Justification Models, the manager will have ready answers for the benefit side of any cost justification model.

---

seems to be different after they have considered the prior steps in the Justification Model. Managers drastically lower the amount of information they consider material after they have evaluated whether it aligns with corporate mission and vision and current corporate priorities. The materiality test could come sooner in the models, but it works most effectively after other tests have been considered.

Corporate Impact

Diligent use of the Identification and Justification Models to this point may have produced several candidates for transformation into real-time information. The final step in the Justification Model is designed to prioritize the few candidates that remain. Very simply, at this stage the impact on the overall corporation needs to be measured and the goals that will have the biggest potential impact should be the first to be pursued. Every piece of information considered at this point is aligned with corporate priorities; the question remains as to which of the manager's goals will have the biggest impact on the corporation.

Specifically for the manager at Consumer Products, Inc., the question may be "What percentage of corporate revenue and corporate profits does my product generate?" If the revenue figure is greater than the profit figure, then information that supports the revenue goal should be at the top of the list. It's also important to consider the possible negative impacts of goals not being met. Particularly if the products, people, or processes that are the manager's responsibility are far upstream in the corporation's overall process flow, the effect of missing goals may be very large indeed in downstream processes and therefore dictate a priority.

Having completed both the Identification and Justification Models, the manager will have a list of the very few metrics that should be monitored in real time properly prioritized. Having used the Identification Model to determine what should be monitored and the Justification Model to determine whether the items are worth monitoring, the vast cloud of information will have been reduced to the 5 percent that will enable predicting the present and real-time opportunity detection. From here the manager can pursue obtaining the information and putting an end to surprises in her business.

real time in the real world

O<small>NE OF THE SENIOR</small> corporate executives I interviewed in the course of my research told me about his new philosophy for managing in an era with so much uncertainty and ambiguity: "It's OK to know what you don't know. What you need is to be able to react faster than anybody else." In stark contrast to this belief, which widely pervades current management thinking, the experiences of many companies show that the key issue is not the ability to respond quickly but the ability to detect changes when they occur.

Predicting the present and real-time opportunity detection will be for corporations what GPS and radar have become in maritime and aviation activities: agents of eliminating surprise. Thanks to new real-time navigation and avionic systems, the largest ocean tankers and largest passenger and cargo planes in the world can fly through the thickest fog in zero visibility with certainty and almost zero ambiguity.

Part 2 directs attention to examining how predicting the present and real-time opportunity detection function in the real world to provide a "heads-up" and eliminate surprises. Chapter 3 examines examples of surprise events where managers missed the opportunity to monitor, capture, or analyze the right information in real time that would have warned of impending problems and how the Identification and Justification Models would have helped reveal this vital information. The suspected events in chapter 4 happened in companies that were monitoring the right information but failing to report it, and as a result were still surprised by a change in their business status. Again, the emphasis is on how real-time opportunity detection would have enabled the companies to avoid disaster. Chapter 5 examines a series of success stories about companies that have surmounted business surprises by putting the right real-time information in the right hands. These stories show the success that is within the grasp of managers who implement predicting the present and real-time opportunity detection to get a heads-up when opportunities or disasters are on the way.

3

surprise events:
missing the warning

Surprise event: The event is not reported, in some cases because it was not monitored, captured, or analyzed.

MORE THAN A DECADE after the fall of the Soviet Union, with international terrorists having firmly replaced communists as national enemies, it's easy to lose sight of how shocking the February 24, 1994, arrest of Aldrich Ames on charges of espionage was. Ames was a fairly high-ranking CIA officer who, it was later revealed, had been spying for the Soviet Union and Russia for more than nine years. While we may never know the full extent of the damage to United States intelligence caused by Ames, the director of the CIA provided Congress with the following partial list of consequences from Ames's spying:

- At least nine U.S. clandestine agents in the Soviet Union were executed.

- The identities of many U.S. agents (from the CIA and other agencies) were disclosed to the Soviets, and later the Russians.

- Techniques and methods of double agent operations as well as details of U.S. counterintelligence activities were revealed.

- Details of U.S. intelligence technical collection activities and analytic techniques were provided.

- Intelligence reports, arms control papers, and selected Department of State and Department of Defense cables were handed over.[1]

Two questions emerge on examining this list: (1) How was it that the CIA allowed a member of their organization to spy for *nine* years? (2) Could the CIA have done anything to stop Ames from becoming a spy in the first place? In fact, the single most important factor that permitted Ames to provide a steady stream of information to U.S. enemies was the absence of monitoring, capture, and analysis (much less reporting) of information related to his activities.

Aldrich Ames began his career in the CIA in 1967. Over the next seventeen years he served in a variety of posts, rarely distinguishing himself. In fact, he was cited by superiors on several occasions for offenses ranging from alcohol abuse to losing his credentials at a softball field to leaving sensitive information in a briefcase that he misplaced on a commuter train. Perhaps the biggest warning event that was not captured took place while he was stationed in Mexico City. Ames became romantically involved with a Mexican woman employed at the Colombian embassy. Ames engaged in the relationship despite being married (his wife was in the United States) and despite explicit rules against such relationships. Even though Ames's colleagues knew of the relationship and the need for Ames to inform his superiors, no one took any remedial actions. Ames showed consistent disregard for rules, procedures, and security precautions throughout his career. The CIA did not capture this information critical to the evaluation of its personnel; as a result, Ames was given access to ever more sensitive information that foreign governments were willing to pay for. By 1985, Ames was back in the United States, divorced, and remarried and was facing growing amounts of debt. It was then that he turned to espionage to supplement his income.[2]

The CIA not only missed capturing evidence of the risk Ames presented before he reached a position of significant responsibility in the counterintelligence department, but it also did not monitor the very clear evidence of Ames's spying once it began:

- Ames spent $1,397,300 between April 1985 and November 1993, even though his salary during that period totaled only $336,164.

- He purchased a used Jaguar, a new Jaguar, and a new Honda.

- He bought a house for more than $540,000, in cash.

- He took expensive personal trips without informing the CIA, as rules dictated.

- His superior discovered that Ames kept secret documents on his PC in violation of CIA policy.[3]

Even the lowest levels of security clearance in the U.S. government require disclosure of items like these (financial statements, foreign trips, and so on), yet the CIA was not monitoring these items for a person with far more than a basic security clearance.

When the CIA finally discovered Ames's treachery, the only response option was jailing him; the time for other steps that would have prevented the deaths of U.S. agents and the compromise of U.S. intelligence was long past. The reports issued in the aftermath of the Ames affair clearly show that if the CIA had been monitoring agents' financial affairs in real time, disaster could easily have been averted.

WorldCom

While spying dominated the national news in February 1994, the business news for much of 2002 was dominated by allegations of fraud and images of former corporate executives in handcuffs. The largest bankruptcy in U.S. history, that of

WorldCom, precipitated by fraud committed by senior executives, was one of the stories plastered across newspapers. Although the Aldrich Ames case was clearly an unnecessary surprise brought about by an absence of monitoring or reporting of key information about an employee of the CIA, can WorldCom and other cases of corporate fraud be considered surprise events—surprises that can be ended through real-time opportunity detection? Perhaps. Let's look closer at the origin of events at WorldCom and other cases.

In the big picture, business fraud originates in many cases because of the surprise of disappointing quarterly or annual results and the exhaustion or absence of legal response options. Rarely is massive fraud the first step. As Greg Rayburn, WorldCom's temporary chief restructuring officer said, "If someone had gone into Scott Sullivan's office and suggested he move billions of dollars from operating expenses to capital expense accounts, he would have thrown them right out of the office. That's not how fraud works."[4] Rayburn reflected that, in his experience, "fraud usually begins a little at a time." The sequence generally begins, he noted, when overwhelming pressure to meet earnings expectations combined with unexpectedly poor quarterly or annual results lead an executive to first reallocate reserves (funds put aside for specific anticipated expenses in the future), believing that these funds can be replaced in the future without damage to the corporation. (Changing reserve amounts is perfectly legal as long as the shift in assumptions allowing such a change is valid and disclosed.) When disappointing results continue to surprise these executives, the critical point hits. The executives believe they must meet expectations and all legal response options have run out. So they turn to small—but progressively larger—illegal manipulations of public accounts to meet expectations.

This is exactly how fraud played out at WorldCom. First, reserves allocated for line costs were reduced. When results continued to fall below expectations over several quarters, line costs, which according to generally accepted accounting principles (GAAP) must be booked as operating expenses, were

FIGURE 3-1

The graph compares WorldCom's reported and actual financial results from 2000 to 2002.

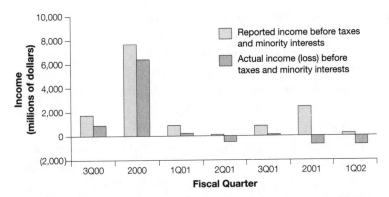

Source: Securities and Exchange Commission, Plaintiff, v. WorldCom, Inc., Defendant. United States District Court, Southern District of New York. Civ. No. 02-CV-4963 (JSR). Available at <http://www.sec. gov/litigation/complaints/comp17829.htm> (accessed 17 February 2003).

shifted to capital expense accounts, changing WorldCom's reported results (figure 3-1).[5]

The role of earnings expectations in this discussion is critical. Fraud that develops along the lines laid out by Rayburn is inseparably linked to the belief that expected goals must be achieved at all costs. Although real-time opportunity detection has no influence over the belief, it can have a marked influence on (a) the expectations that are set in the first place and (b) the response options available for ensuring that expectations are met. Before going further, we need to briefly discuss the role of consensus earnings estimates in today's public companies.

Consensus Earnings Estimates

When any company decides to raise capital in public stock markets by selling shares, it not only prepares to meet regulatory requirements, it hires an investment bank (or banks) to represent it in the financial markets. The analysts of the main underwriting investment bank or of other banks involved often assist in the selling of the company's stock by issuing a research report that reviews the prospects and other data about the company and most important, enumerates future revenues and earnings of the company in the opinion of the analyst. If the stock becomes widely traded, more and more analysts from more and more firms issue reports. These reports are heavily influenced by the stated expectations of the company's management as well as the analysts' confidence in the expectations in the face of prevailing market conditions. The research reports are often blended together to determine the *consensus earnings estimate* for a company.

How important are consensus estimates to a company's standing in financial markets? Consider the case of Williams-Sonoma, which announced its year-end 2001 results on March 11, 2002. The company reported earnings per diluted share of $1.20, just one penny short of the $1.21 per diluted share consensus estimates of securities analysts. Despite favorable market conditions leading up to the day of its earnings announcement, Williams-Sonoma shares lost more than $150 million dollars in market capitalization by the end of March 11 (table 3-1). In the market's eyes, it apparently did not matter that the company reported a nearly 17 percent increase in net sales, a 58 percent increase in net earnings, and a 52 percent increase in earnings per diluted share during fourth quarter 2001 versus fourth quarter 2000. The loss in market value that day due to missing consensus estimates by a penny was equivalent to 19 percent of the company's fiscal 2001 revenues.

Of course, this is just one example of the effect of missing earnings estimates posted by securities analysts. But it does indicate how thousands of companies have fared over many years if they failed to meet the earnings projections compiled by analysts. As former chairman of the Securities and Exchange Commission Arthur Levitt lamented in 1998, "While the problem . . . is not new, it has swelled in a market that is unforgiving of companies that miss their estimates. I recently read of one major U.S. company, that failed to meet its so-called 'numbers' by one penny, and lost more than six percent of its stock value in one day."[6] The problem seems only to have grown worse.

TABLE 3-1

Fall of Williams-Sonoma's Stock Price After Missing Earnings Expectations by Just a Penny

Index/Stock	March 8, 2002	March 11, 2002
Dow Jones Industrials	10572.49, up 47.12	10611.24, up 38.35
Nasdaq Composite	1926.67, up 45.04	1929.49, up 2.82
S&P 500	1164.31, up 6.77	1168.26, up 3.95
Williams-Sonoma stock price	$49.04, down $.58	$46.40, down $2.64

Changing the Game

Real-time opportunity detection *can* influence (a) the earnings expectations that are set and (b) the response options available for ensuring that expectations are met, thereby reducing the number of times an executive has to report the potentially devastating news of not reaching earnings estimates. The critical first small steps toward fraud are brought about by the combination of the market power of earnings estimates with the surprise actual results are to most executives. They do not know what their final results will be until well after the quarter has closed because real-time monitoring, capture, and analysis of the elements that make up the results are not taking place. By this time, other response options are impossible.

WorldCom in its heyday was a growth stock, its value dependent on a constantly growing top line (if not always a growing bottom line). This growth was critical to the company, whose strategy included using its appreciated stock as currency to acquire other companies to grow revenue further. CEO Bernard Ebbers would highlight growth of revenues and the stock price in *all* his discussions with shareholders and the investment community. For instance, in January 2000, he related that "$100 invested in MCI WorldCom in 1989 would be worth $7,240 today."[7] However, despite the priority of growing revenue, WorldCom was monitoring neither its customers nor the surrounding economy for signs of declining demand.

Thus, when revenue began to slip, taking executives by surprise, the company slipped toward fraud. It was all too easy a path for a company so focused on growth.

There is a lesson in the WorldCom experience for managers in high-growth companies where pressure to meet revenue expectations is particularly high (because a high percentage of the perceived value of the company's stock is tied up in belief of continuing growth). Growth companies in particular must, upon answering the first and second questions of the Identification Model (goals and priority) with "revenue," begin evaluating how to monitor revenue in real time.

Consider the real-time evolution model as it looks for many executives (figure 3-2). It shows a surprise event where informa-

FIGURE 3-2

If a revenue shortfall is not captured in real time, valuable response options become impossible, leaving only highly unpalatable choices that can encourage fraud.

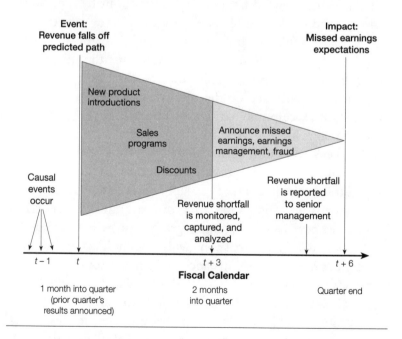

tion about revenue is not monitored, captured, and analyzed in real time and is only reported simultaneously with the impact of the event, long after any operational responses can correct the revenue shortfall and change the impact. If the event of revenue falling short is being monitored and reported in real time, there will be many options (for example, new product introductions, sales programs and incentives, discounts) open to management to reverse the decline. They will have many choices other than simply announcing at the end of the quarter that revenue targets were not met, and the temptation to start on the road to fraud will never arise as management's ability to meet targets despite unfavorable trends increases.

In a broader context, figure 3-2 also illustrates the time frames of reporting. According to SEC regulations, companies have thirty days after the end of the quarter to report quarterly results; this is typically when executives issue guidance for the next quarter. When the correct information is being monitored, captured, and analyzed, executives have one third of the current quarter's results already in hand, allowing them to provide much more accurate guidance on the eventual results of the quarter. Thus, a virtuous cycle is created. Management is more able to meet expectations because of real-time opportunity detection. As expectations are met, management's credibility in guiding expectations is enhanced. Analysts are more likely to trust the expectations that management has set and the consensus earnings estimates set by analysts will be closer to management's guidance. Continuing to use real-time opportunity detection, management is again better able to meet the more accurate earnings expectations, and yet again management's credibility is enhanced.

Thus, real-time opportunity detection cannot guarantee the absence of fraud, but it can reduce the likelihood of fraud as revenue-related surprise events are eliminated. Companies that engage in real-time opportunity detection can also achieve significant market valuation advantages over competitors as the market rewards the company's ability to consistently meet expectations.

National Century Financial Enterprises

Regardless of what real-time opportunity detection can reveal, there will always be managers who step outside the law to achieve their own personal goals. The fallout from the fraud they commit extends well beyond these managers and the companies they ruin. Losses and liabilities affect potentially all the company's partners and customers. Although real-time opportunity detection cannot stop every instance of fraud, it can lessen the impact on a company of the surprise of learning that a key partner or supplier is bent on criminal activity.

Consider the situation at National Century Financial Enterprises (NCFE) in 2002 and 2003. Before filing for Chapter 11 bankruptcy reorganization in November 2002, National Century was one of the largest providers of working capital to small health care providers. National Century would buy accounts receivable at a discount from health care providers who needed cash to fund daily operations and could not wait the weeks and often months it takes for insurance companies and Medicare to pay claims. NCFE would in turn sell the accounts receivable as asset-backed bonds, repaying the bonds as the payments were received from insurers. The bond sales were backed by banking firms such as Credit Suisse First Boston, Bank One, and J. P. Morgan Chase, who required, in the bond covenants, that certain amounts of cash always be available for repayment of the bonds.

Over the years, National Century sold billions of dollars' worth of bonds. As early as 1999, however, financial troubles began to occur at the company. An FBI and SEC investigation is still continuing, but it appears that executives of the company may have been misdirecting funds to health care providers they owned a stake in. As a result, National Century began experiencing a cash crisis. Internal memos documented a growing gap between the amount of cash in hand and the amount required by the existing bond covenants. In November 1999, the total gap had exceeded $100 million. Despite this, the company succeeded in offering $2 billion of new bonds between 1999 and 2002.

How is it that a company that did not have enough funds to meet its present obligations with banks was backed to sell even more? Very simply, the company began moving cash from one account to another, even daily, so that when the banks checked for compliance with covenants, it appeared that requirements were met.[8] This was possible only because the accounts were being monitored not in real time but only at specific intervals. Real-time monitoring of the accounts would have allowed NCFE's backers to easily capture the transfer of funds and determine the need to "fire" NCFE as a customer of their bond services.

Instead, CSFB, Bank One and JPMorgan Chase are now being sued by groups of investors who bought the NCFE bonds that the banks vouched for.[9] The lawsuit is asking difficult questions about the way the banks conducted business with NCFE. As securities law professor John Coffee puts it (inspired by Watergate), "What did CSFB know and when did they know it?"[10] Even if the banks are ultimately found to be not liable, the result is nevertheless a tremendous embarrassment to an industry already plagued by the Enron and stock research scandals. Damage to reputations, of course, spills over into future business. The ability of the asset-backed securities divisions of these banks to win business from other companies seeking to sell bonds in this market depends heavily on the market's perception of their reliability.[11] The companies are caught now between legal penalties if they knew the situation at NCFE and did nothing and being perceived as "asleep at the switch" if they did not. In the aftermath of the story, Moody's, one of the leading bond-rating firms, has clarified that its ratings assume that the companies in the role assumed by CSFB and others are monitoring reserve accounts.[12] In this light, there is no question that the status of the bank accounts of NCFE (or any other client) would pass the Identification and Justification Models. Generating revenue is a high-priority goal, the ability to generate revenue depends on trust, and trust depends on the integrity of current bond offerings. Here is a causal event of revenue that would provide adequate response time to not become involved with a suspect company in the first place or at the very least blow the whistle first and be perceived as a trustworthy organization.

This monitoring dictated by the Identification and Justification Models would not, of course, require someone to be assigned to watching account statuses twenty-four hours a day. Just as the TCAS system used by airline pilots does not require pilots to constantly monitor the surrounding airspace, a system of simple automated alarms that would inform managers of account activity that falls outside the expected norms is all that is necessary.

It's hard to understand why large banks did not undertake real-time monitoring of this sort (after all, you and I can monitor our own bank accounts in real time today) until we consider that the processes in place were those that were created when real-time monitoring was not possible. In many cases the gap between an event and its monitoring, capture, and reporting seems to stem primarily from a failure to update inherited processes and business practices. The processes and practices of the past were dictated by the technology available at the time and have not been revised as technology has advanced. The result, as always, is needless and harmful distance from event to reporting. The result in the case of National Century was a classic surprise event. The information could easily have been monitored in real time by the banks but was not; it may be years before the bond traders emerge from the cloud of doubt created by National Century's default.

Monitoring information in real time is not enough, however. One of the reasons that the National Century situation is so interesting is that the financial industry monitors, captures, analyzes, and reports in real time on thousands of categories of information each day. It is not just the monitoring, capture, and analysis of information that assures success; as the Identification Model illustrates and National Century demonstrates, to avoid surprise events you must be monitoring the right information. Of course, it is not just the financial industry that is vulnerable to missing the right information.

Commercial Airline Industry

The news from the airline industry since September 2001 is harrowing. Two major U.S. carriers have filed for bankruptcy, and several international carriers have ceased operations altogether. Announced losses are in the tens of billions of dollars. Thousands of flight attendants, pilots, and other personnel have been furloughed indefinitely. Many point to the chilling effects of September 11 on air travel as a cause of the industry's woes, but the truth is that the problems began well before the terrorist attacks; many of the problems are the result of poor decisions caused in part by a lack of real-time information. This may seem strange because the airline industry monitors mountains of real-time information: ticket sales, passenger enplanements, baggage loaded, flight status, and gate arrival times, among a hundred other kinds of information. However, the airline industry was a victim of a surprise event because it was not monitoring the right information in real time, the information that is revealed by the Identification Model.

One of the key ways to track the health of the airline industry is a metric known as revenue passenger miles. Revenue passenger miles are the number of miles paying passengers flew (they exclude frequent flier award tickets, for instance). From the beginning of 1996 through the second quarter of 2001, the metric was growing steadily, generally from 1 percent to 3 percent from quarter to quarter (figure 3-3). Although sustained profits have always been hard to come by in the airline industry, many airlines were announcing record levels of revenue and operating profits in 1999. The year 2000 proved to be a difficult one because nearly every major airline was negotiating for a new contract with one of the major unions (pilots, flight attendants, and mechanics). However, revenue passenger miles continued to grow. In this environment, in August of 2000, United Airlines signed what was described as "the most expensive pilot contract ever negotiated," which provided pay increases of up to 30 percent.[13] Combined with a subsequent deal with the machinists' union, the contracts led to an estimated $1 billion annualized cost increase.[14] In the spring of 2001, Delta Airlines signed a new contract with its pilots that topped even the United deal—a contract that would provide wage hikes up to 63 percent by 2005 and would cost Delta an estimated $2.4 billion.[15] To put these numbers in perspective, note that personnel costs account for roughly one third of the airline industry's expenses. Clearly such contracts could have been signed only in expectation of in-

FIGURE 3-3

Airlines' revenue passenger miles fell dramatically in 2001 after years of growth.

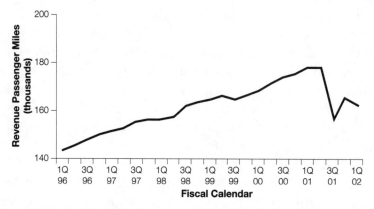

Source: U.S. Department of Transportation, Bureau of Transportation Statistics, "Air Traffic Statistics and Airline Financial Statistics," <http://www.bts.gov/oai/indicators/sysopfinan.html> (accessed 12 November 2002).

creasing revenue. Another indicator of the airlines' expectations can be seen in the more than 600 orders for new planes from Boeing's Commercial Aircraft Group, more than Boeing had anticipated.[16]

Given the overall state of the industry at the time, these moves seemed to make sense. How could airline executives and managers have anticipated the chilling effect on air travel of September 11, 2001? The drastic decline in passengers was nowhere in sight at the time. Despite damage done by several labor strikes, total industry operating revenues continued to grow through the first quarter of 2001 (figure 3-4). Although the industry was tracking ticket sales and many other operating metrics in real time, it could not have foreseen the drastic changes to come. Or could it?

The airline industry illustrates how important it is to follow the Identification Model through the necessary iterations to find information to track that will give enough warning of future impact to allow for effective responses. A high proportion of expenses in the airline industry are fixed over time due to

FIGURE 3-4

Airline industry total operating revenues peaked in the first quarter of 2001, well before the September 11 attacks.

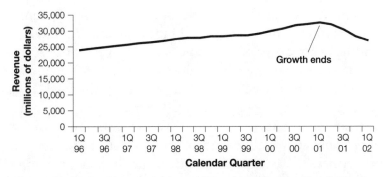

Source: U.S. Department of Transportation, Bureau of Transportation Statistics, "System Operating Financials," <http://www.bts.gov/oai/indicators/sysopfinan.html> (accessed 12 November 2002).

items like labor contracts, aircraft purchases (which are financed and paid over time), and jet fuel (which is often purchased well in advance to flatten out price fluctuations). For many industries, tracking total operating revenues in real time, which the airline industry is close to doing, would allow sufficient lag before impact for appropriate responses. Due to the fixed cost structure, however, operating revenue in real time did not provide adequate warning for the airline industry. By the time operating revenue decreases were evident, cost increases were already locked in.

If we look at causal events of operating revenue, as the Identification Model dictates when response options do not fit in the event–impact lag, we find other candidates for real-time monitoring. The largest component of operating revenue for the major airlines is business travel. As anyone who has traveled on fully refundable, three-day advance fares knows, you can often find yourself sitting beside someone who paid more than 75 percent less than you did for the same ticket (especially frustrating if they have the aisle seat while you're stuck in the middle!). Because most business travel arrangements are made with short lead times, however, simply tracking business travel would not significantly increase the event–impact lag. The Identification Model would dictate taking another step backward in the event–impact chain to the events that have the greatest impact on business travel.

Clearly, the largest factor that determines the amount of business travel is the overall state of the economy. We also know that the major driver of economic growth in the late 1990s was spending on information technology. In the graph in figure 3-5, you can see that spending on information technology began slowing in the spring of 2000, a full year before operating revenue at the airlines turned negative but critically before the labor contracts were signed and before most of the orders for new planes were placed. If there is any doubt about the importance of the economy to the airline industry, Delta CEO Leo Mullin clarifies: "An unfortunate reality for our industry is that, since business travel expenses are an early cost-cutting target, airlines suffer a disproportionate amount of revenue pain during these cycles relative to the rest of the business world."[17]

In fairness to the airlines, we must note that the figures for IT spending were not being released in real time, and the figures became known only several quarters later. However, the airlines had the information in their hands that would have al-

FIGURE 3-5

IT spending peaked in the second quarter of 2000, before airlines negotiated new labor contracts.

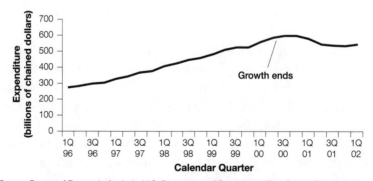

Source: Bureau of Economic Analysis, U.S. Department of Commerce, "Real Private Fixed Investment by Type," National Income and Products Accounts, 30 May 2003, <http://www.bea.gov/bea/dn/nipaweb/TableViewFixed.asp#Mid> (accessed 10 June 2003).

lowed them to see the slowdown sooner than the rest of the economy. According to Delta Airlines economist Eric Amel, one of the key metrics that an airline tracks is travel by corporate account. Tracking travel activity of corporate accounts allows airlines to offer discounts and other programs to companies who use their services regularly. Despite this tracking, however, Delta does not convert from corporate account to industry sector (using Standard Industry Code [SIC] or North American Industry Classification System [NAICS] codes).[18]

Had Delta tracked passengers by industry or U.S. Department of Labor occupational titles, for instance, airlines could have seen the declining trend in travel by IT companies and IT personnel and predicted the present state of that sector of the economy. In turn, the airlines would have been able to draw conclusions about the state of the overall economy and its future prospects for business travel and to avoid the surprise event they encountered (figure 3-6). Real-time opportunity detection would not have prepared the airlines for the drop in travel

FIGURE 3-6

By the time the airlines noticed the decline in business travel, they had already locked in higher fixed costs.

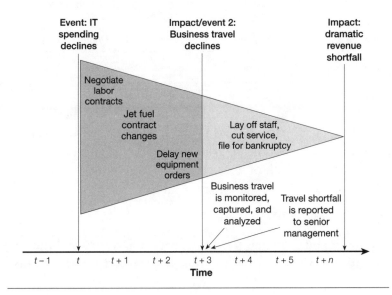

TABLE 3-2

Identification Model for the Airline Industry

Highest priority goal	Operating profit
Causal events	Revenue from business travel; state of economy
Metric	Travel by industry
Response options available	Negotiate labor contracts, jet fuel purchase contracts; defer purchase of new equipment

TABLE 3-3

Justification Model for the Airline Industry

Align with corporate mission/vision	Yes. (Delta's vision: "We will provide value and distinctive products to our customers, a *superior return for investors,* and challenging and rewarding work for Delta people in an environment that respects and values their contributions.") [italics added]
Align with priorities	Yes. (From speech by Delta CEO Leo Mullen, June 2002: "Second, Delta is managing the *continuing revenue lag* by effectively *controlling what can be controlled—costs, capacity, and liquidity;* leveraging key advantages; and making smart, disciplined investment decisions.") [italics added]
Materiality	In reaction to current events between 2001 and 2002, Delta significantly altered its jet fuel purchase patterns and reduced aircraft capacity by 11 percent.
Corporate impact	Personnel costs represent one third of industry costs.

caused by the terrorist attacks, but it could have prevented the airlines from being as overextended as they were when the attacks happened (tables 3-2 and 3-3). Already at the breaking point because of overhead costs, the attacks brought the airline industry to the brink of disaster.

Ending Surprise Events

The foregoing examples from the financial industry and the airline industry show how far we have to go to end surprise events.

Ending business surprises depends on determining the right information to monitor and setting up the processes and procedures for monitoring, capturing, and analyzing changes in that information. The airline and financial industries arguably monitor more real-time information than all other industries combined, yet they are still victims of surprise events. Although the case for real-time information is relatively straightforward, these examples clearly show that simply making the case for real-time information is not enough; monitoring the right information is the only way to end business surprises.

4

suspected events: reporting too late

Suspected event: The event is monitored, captured, and analyzed but reported too late for effective action.

IMAGINE FOR A MOMENT Henry Wadsworth Longfellow's famous poem "Paul Revere's Ride" with a slightly different scenario. Revere had arranged for real-time monitoring, capture, and analysis of British troop movements in Boston. However, once he received this real-time information, rather than acting immediately, he spent several hours shoeing his horse and getting dressed for his ride. If Revere had behaved this way, by the time he reached the towns of Middlesex County, his warnings of the approach of the British would have come too late. Or imagine that rather than crying out a warning to the inhabitants of each town, he had simply nailed a letter to the front door of the town church for the townsfolk to read in the morning. Each of these scenarios seems patently ridiculous, but neither is far from reality. A rider named William Dawes set out from Boston at the same time as Revere with the same news, but did not stir the famous response that led to the battles at Concord and Lexington. Why? Because he failed to report his information to the right people.[1]

The imagined delays and Dawes's experience are similar to the situation encountered by many enterprises today: Even when they have the facilities for monitoring, capturing, and analyzing the right real-time information, they do not report it in real time. These companies are tracking critical business information in real time but are still the victims of unanticipated problems or lost opportunities.

Determining what information to monitor, capture, and analyze in real time is only the beginning. The real-time information must be reported to the right parties and reported while appropriate and effective response options are still possible. Without reporting in time for effective responses, the monitoring of critical business information is worthless.

Herein lies the reason that so few have heard of the DEW Line. Although it was a marvel when it was completed in the early 1950s, by the mid-1960s it was no longer useful. Delivery of nuclear weapons had evolved from bombs carried by airplanes to warheads carried by intercontinental ballistic missiles (ICBMs). An incoming missile could be detected by the DEW Line as the missile crossed the North Pole, but the missiles traveled so fast that even with instantaneous reporting, no response options were possible. It is unlikely that the detection of a missile aimed for Washington, D.C., by the DEW Line would have given sufficient warning for even a presidential authorization of a counterstrike. Thus, the DEW Line of radar installations gave way to a comprehensive network of satellites that could detect a missile launch anywhere in the Soviet Union the moment it happened. While the response options were limited to one—launching a counterstrike—the option was a deterrent to the missiles being launched in the first place.

Not reporting in time for sufficient response played a role in the largest corporate scandal of 2002. One of the best-known anecdotes of the Enron scandal is that of Sherron Watkins's anonymous memo to Ken Lay as he reassumed the role of CEO, following Jeff Skilling's resignation for "personal reasons." In the memo, Ms. Watkins reported to Mr. Lay what she considered to be highly suspect financial dealings—bogus off-balance-sheet partnerships designed not to hedge risk but to improve the look of Enron's books.[2] The memo and Ms. Watkins's assistance in the forensic accounting investigation earned her honors as one of *Time* magazine's People of the Year, but the document reported the problems far too late for any response to stop or clean up the fraudulent financial dealings of the firm without tens of thousands of people losing their jobs and/or retirement savings. This is a consistent theme in many business surprises. Managers who could act to prevent problems do not receive the necessary information until too late. Such was the case at Boeing in the late 1990s.

Boeing

Like much of the U.S. industrial sector, Boeing was suffering in the mid-1990s. After enjoying commercial aircraft revenues of $25 billion in 1993, revenues fell below $20 billion in 1994 and sank further to $17.5 billion in 1995. In Boeing's 1995 10K filing with the Securities and Exchange Commission, the company stated:

> The declines in revenue for the past two years were due to fewer commercial jet transport deliveries as a result of economic conditions and airline industry overcapacity in most major market areas of the world. Additionally, a ten-week strike during the fourth quarter of 1995 by the International Association of Machinists and Aerospace Workers (IAM) resulted in the delay of about 30 jet transport deliveries representing approximately $2 billion in reduced sales in 1995.[3]

From 1993 to 1995, total deliveries of commercial jets had fallen from 330 to 206 airplanes (table 4-1).

Although deliveries hit bottom in 1995, the prospects that year were looking brighter. As the economic recovery took hold, the airline industry, led by carriers in Asia, began ordering

TABLE 4-1

Boeing Aircraft Deliveries by Model, 1993–1995

	1993	1994	1995
737	152	121	89
747	56	40	25
757	71	69	43
767	51	40	36
777	—	—	13
Total	330	270	206

Source: Boeing 10K Report, 1995, <http://www.sec.gov/Archives/edgar/data/12927/0000012927-96-000003.txt> (accessed 28 December 2002), 23.

planes to replace their aging fleets.[4] In 1996, Boeing was facing the seemingly enviable problem of not having sufficient resources to meet the rapid increases in aircraft orders. By the end of 1997, four months after Boeing and rival McDonnell Douglas had merged, new orders (for both companies) had risen to 504 aircraft and deliveries had reached 374 planes (table 4-2).

Given the run-up in orders, it looked as if Boeing's third quarter 1997 report would be record setting. However, rather than reporting record revenues and profits, Boeing instead announced the largest loss in the company's history:

> Third quarter earnings were reduced by approximately $1.6 billion pretax, or $1.0 billion after tax, representing the financial impact of the unplanned and abnormal production inefficiencies and late-delivery costs associated with the accelerated production increases on the 7-series commercial aircraft programs.[5]

In addition to the $1.6 billion charge in the third quarter, Boeing estimated that it would need to charge a further $1 billion over the next four quarters.

TABLE 4-2

Boeing Aircraft Deliveries by Model, 1995–1997

	1995	1996	1997
737	89	76	135
747	25	26	39
757	43	42	46
767	36	42	41
777	13	32	59
MD-80	—	12	16
MD-90	—	24	26
MD-11	—	15	12
Total	206	269	374

Source: Boeing, 1997 Annual Report, <http://www.boeing.com/company/offices/financial/finreports/annual/97annualreport/commerci.htm> (accessed 28 December 2002).

The story of this huge surprise at Boeing is as complicated as the process of building jet aircraft, but in the end we see once again the challenges of management without real-time information. In a 2001 interview, Boeing CEO Phil Condit commented on the importance of information in making difficult decisions: "Do I lose sleep over [decisions]? No. Because these decisions are made with knowledge. If I had to make them blindly, yes I would lose sleep."[6] In 1996 and 1997, Boeing senior executives were making decisions with knowledge but knowledge only of the past; they had only estimates of the present, which, as measured by the result, is not much better than making decisions blind. Unlike the airline industry in 2000, at Boeing the cause of the problem was not missing the correct real-time information to monitor; it was failing to report real-time information on parts shortages and production problems to senior managers until it was too late for any response but a shutdown of production lines and a massive charge against earnings.

What Happened at Boeing?

Building airplanes is certainly one of the most complex manufacturing tasks being carried out today. Each airplane requires thousands of precisely engineered parts fitted together by highly trained mechanics and technicians in precisely the right order. In fact at Boeing, according to Ron Woodard, president of Boeing Commercial Airplane Group, completing the tasks required to assemble an aircraft out of order (known as "out-of-sequence assembly") costs five times more than doing the same work in the proper order.[7] Thus, having the right parts on hand at the right time is crucial for cost control. When there are relatively few planes to produce, as there were in 1995, this wasn't a problem for Boeing. As new orders came flooding in, however, the company attempted to move from delivering fewer than twenty new planes per month to delivering more than forty.[8]

Boeing had encountered problems when attempting a similar rapid production ramp-up in the past. In nearly identical circumstances in the 1980s, Boeing had struggled to increase production capacity and "lost opportunities because we were very conservative," according to Woodard. Recognizing that the slump of the 1990s was part of a standard business cycle and that an upturn similar to that of the 1980s would come eventually, the company took a number of actions to prevent missing opportunities due to similar problems in ramping up deliveries in the future. For instance, the company dramatically reduced the number of suppliers it used, cutting their numbers nearly in half, believing that this would make order and inventory management more efficient.[9] Additionally, the company rolled out a new consolidated parts management system, known as DCAC, that cost nearly $1 billion but was expected to pay for itself in two years because the time to produce an airplane would be cut dramatically—specifically by minimizing parts shortages and out-of-sequence work.[10]

In reality, however, the moves Boeing managers took to cut costs and achieve production efficiencies had exactly the opposite effect. The software was bug-riddled and was producing more errors than cost savings. As reported by *Business Week*, despite a report from internal auditor Susan Parker that "no [managers at Boeing's Wichita assembly plant] would sign off" on the estimated cost savings of DCAC in March of 1997, the estimated cost savings numbers were passed on to senior management for inclusion in their business plans.[11] Additionally, when Boeing's rapidly rising orders for planes led inescapably to rapidly rising orders for parts, many suppliers could not keep up with the increased demand. While order management was greatly simplified by rationalizing suppliers, Boeing underestimated suppliers' sensitivity to the last downturn in demand. The suppliers decided not to invest in capacity until the new boom was proven to be lasting. As a result, the suppliers could not meet demand and there were no backup suppliers to order parts from.[12] While senior management continued to make strategic plans based on estimated costs (with the built-in savings), managers in assembly plants saw parts shortages, schedule overruns, and out-of-sequence jobs continue to grow (figure 4-1). The managers saw in real time the problems that were being encountered. Each day they went to work they saw more and more out-of-sequence work being performed due to parts shortages and inventory management problems. However, despite this real-time knowl-

FIGURE 4-1

The number of jobs behind schedule in the 737 and 747 programs at Boeing in 1997 kept growing.

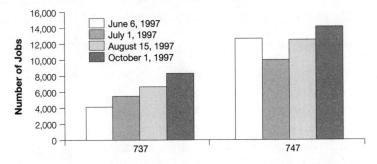

Source: Decision on Motion to Dismiss Case No. C97-1715Z Class Action Order, United States District Court, Western District of Washington, Seattle [filed 8 September 1998]. Jobs Behind Schedule Chart, <http://securities.stanford.edu/1012/BA97/order.html> (accessed 15 February 2003).

edge of production problems, no effective process was in place for passing the information on to senior executives in real time.

One clear symptom of the absence of real-time reporting was a meeting that took place at Boeing just three days before the end of the second quarter of 1997, where a number of managers learned that fifteen planes were highly unlikely to be delivered on time. On-time delivery was (and still is) crucial to Boeing's financial results because late deliveries obligated Boeing to make substantial penalty payments to the airlines that had ordered the planes and jeopardized future orders because of the disruption of airlines' plans that late deliveries caused.

Despite the clearly escalating problems in the spring of 1997, senior management did not grasp the scope of the production crisis until the fall. "August was tough but September was the canary in our mine," according to Ron Woodard, meaning that senior executives realized that parts shortages were so severe and out-of-sequence work so out of hand that even an unlimited amount of overtime would not correct the problems.[13] The only response option available when the scale of the problems finally reached senior executives was to shut down production of both the 737 and 757 lines for twenty days to allow the replenishment of parts inventories. Shortly thereafter, Boeing announced its stunning $2.6 billion charges.

The depth of the problem that sprang from an absence of real-time reporting is illustrated by Woodard's choice of analogy. Canaries were the real-time reporting system for miners into the 1900s. They died quickly from exposure to otherwise invisible poison gases in the mines, warning miners of the presence of the toxic substances so that the miners could evacuate. The canaries of Boeing's senior executives lived long after the "poison gas" of parts shortages and out-of-sequence assembly choked Boeing's production processes.

Early information on the problems would have been especially helpful at a company like Boeing because of GAAP accounting rules used in the aerospace industry. The accounting method used, known as program accounting, recognizes that the vast majority of costs in building airplanes, satellites, and the like are taken up front during the design, testing, and initial manufacturing runs. As more units of a particular model are pro-duced, costs drop dramatically. Program accounting allows the costs to be spread over the length of time a particular line will be built; but it therefore requires good estimates of the number of planes that will be built and the cost savings that will be incurred as production experience and efficiency are gained. These esti-mates obviously can become wildly divergent from reality if pro-duction problems are encountered early in an airplane program's life, exactly as it happened at Boeing in the late 1990s.[14]

It may seem easy to conclude that Boeing's management ini-tiatives in the mid-1990s—supplier rationalization and DCAC—were the cause of the $1.6 billion charge. The real problem was not in these initiatives, which theoretically made sense, but in the senior executives' lack of knowledge that in practice they were hurting the short-term production situation. What could managers have done differently if they had known about the problems in real time? One option would have been to limit the number of orders, but this is impractical in the airplane business. Airlines must invest huge amounts of resources in training me-chanics and pilots on a particular plane, so turning away orders because of limited production capacity in the short term could have been disastrous for Boeing in the long term if airlines took their orders to Airbus Industrie, Boeing's rival in the commer-cial jet business. Therefore, it is very possible that problems could not have been avoided entirely. However, greater senior management attention to the problems with DCAC and cer-tainly attention to identifying suppliers for parts with critical shortages may have significantly reduced the impact and dura-tion of the production meltdown. Even less lengthy production shutdowns earlier in time would have lessened the cost to the company (table 4-3).

A larger lesson emerges from the Boeing experience for man-agers who rely heavily on estimates, such as for strategic plan-ning. One key strategic planning tool for situations where the future is uncertain and therefore estimates are required is the contingent road map. A contingent road map specifies several possible courses of action with specific triggers for taking one course rather than another as time passes and actual information

TABLE 4-3

Identification and Justification Models for Boeing

Identification

Highest-priority goal	Delivering airplanes on time and on budget
Causal events	Parts shortages; out-of-sequence work
Metric	Parts inventories; out-of-sequence jobs; jobs behind schedule
Response options available	Greater focus on implementation of parts management system; expanding supplier base

Justification

Alignment with corporate mission/vision	Yes. Boeing's vision and mission statements refer to achieving aerospace leadership (delivering planes on time and on budget is a requirement for leadership) and shareholder value.
Alignment with priorities	Yes. Boeing's stated core competencies include large-scale systems integration and values include customer satisfaction. Both are in jeopardy from production problems.
Materiality	Boeing executives would have acted to prevent late delivery of planes and avoid loss of profit and reputation.
Corporate impact	Commercial airplanes are one of the top three revenue generators for Boeing.

replaces estimates.[15] For instance, Boeing could have had a contingent road map that specified critical levels of parts shortages that would trigger action to reengage suppliers that had been dropped. A contingent road map works best when the information that prompts a particular course is reported in real time. As managers make strategic plans based on estimates of future costs, revenues, and so on, they should consider whether a process exists for reporting in real time whether those estimates hold true. As former Citigroup CEO John Reed noted, when explaining the importance of ensuring that estimates used in strategic planning were constantly updated to reflect current realities, "The most important thing is to ensure that the world doesn't change without your being aware of it."[16] When it does, the result is often a suspected event.

Sears

Sometimes senior executives are aware of the changes in the world around them but a suspected event still occurs, as it did in October 2002 at Sears.

In the world of retailing, where sales are heavily influenced by passing trends and the industry is increasingly dominated by three players who have risen to prominence in the last twenty years, Sears has stood the test of time. Sears, Roebuck and Co. issued its first catalog more than a hundred years ago. Without a knowledge of its history, however, examination of Sears's books in 2002 might have led to the conclusion that Sears was a credit card company that dabbled in retail—the credit division accounted for 60 percent of operating income in 2001. The surprisingly large credit division was at the root of Sears's fall 2002 earnings surprise. At the close of the third quarter of fiscal 2002, Sears not only missed expectations for profitability, it announced a loss due to the need to write off $222 million of bad debt from its credit card business (figure 4-2).

FIGURE 4-2

Sears's uncollectible account provisions rose dramatically in the third quarter of 2002.

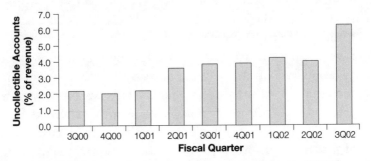

Source: Sears Form 10Q, 2000 to 2002, <http://www.sec.gov/Archives/edgar/data/319256/000095013702006132/c72860e10vq.htm> (accessed 29 January 2003).

For long-time Sears watchers, the announcement must have seemed oddly familiar. Sears's reliance on revenue from its credit division had been growing for years. Caught between the discounters like Wal-Mart and Target, high-end department stores like Macy's, and home improvement warehouses like Home Depot and Lowe's, Sears's retail sales have remained stagnant since the early 1990s. In the mid-1990s, CEO Arthur Martinez, after successfully cutting overhead costs but failing to spur merchandise sales, turned to the credit business to increase growth. However, Sears stumbled badly in 1997 as it realized that it had been overaggressive in extending credit, and defaults surged. Martinez gave current CEO Alan Lacy the task of bringing order to the credit division and putting the business back on a firm footing.[17] Lacy's success paved the way for his ascension to the CEO position when Martinez retired in December 2000. Despite the recent trouble with credit cards, the Sears board signaled its commitment to the credit business by choosing Lacy over other candidates with more experience and success in growing merchandise sales.[18]

Like his predecessor, Lacy saw a great deal of potential in growing the credit card department. When he assumed the role of CEO, he turned over the reins of the credit division to Keven T. Keleghan. Lacy planned to use the profitability from lending to pay for initiatives to get the company's retail sales growing again—initiatives including redesigning stores, introducing new, more stylish clothing lines, and the acquisition of catalog retailer Lands' End. The major step taken by Lacy and Keleghan was to introduce a Sears MasterCard (as opposed to the store's exclusive card). Although the Sears MasterCard was successful, it did not appear to be meeting revenue goals—users were carrying well below the average balance for the industry on their Sears MasterCards. In early 2002, Sears took steps to cover the revenue shortfall, primarily raising rates and fees on the traditional Sears Card to levels well above competitive offerings.[19]

The ability of Sears to draw more fees from these customers hinted that the Sears credit portfolio was once again vulnerable to delinquencies. Cardholders' willingness to pay Sears above-market fees indicated that many of these customers could not get credit elsewhere and were at risk of not paying on their accounts. Indeed, throughout 2001, Sears Card delinquencies were trending up (figure 4-3); the amount of credit held by cardholders who declared bankruptcy increased 20 percent in the third quarter.[20] The continuing economic slump also made it likely that delinquency rates would rise further. According to the Sears PR department, the company was monitoring this trend daily, as well they should, given the credit division's contribution to the company's bottom line.

So if Sears was monitoring the rising delinquency rates and there were signs that the portfolio carried significant risk, why was there a need to surprise investors by increasing allowances for delinquencies by 50 percent in one quarter? Alan Lacy provided a hint in an interview with the *New York Times:* "Keven [Keleghan] did something that was unacceptable in the third quarter. He was not forthcoming about what was happening in his business."[21] In other words, while real-time monitoring of a critical component of the business was happening, it was not

FIGURE 4-3

The delinquency rates of Sears credit card and Sears MasterCard holders in 2001 and 2002 highlight the growing credit quality problems in the Sears portfolio.

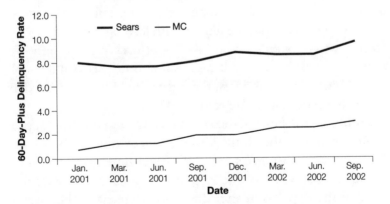

Source: Sears Form 10Q for the period ending 28 September 2002, <http://www.sec.gov/Archives/edgar/data/319256/000095013702006132/c72860e10vq.htm> (accessed 29 January 2003).

being reported to the one executive in the company most able to take effective action.

At Boeing, the suspected event was caused by an absence of process for reporting real-time information to senior executives. At Sears, the president of the credit division himself had access to real-time information on delinquencies in the credit business. However, if we look again at the Identification and Justification Models, it becomes apparent why a suspected event took place at Sears. Consider the goals at Sears (maximizing operating income to fund sales growth initiatives) and the response options available to the president of the credit division as real-time information on delinquencies was delivered. Sears does not write off debts until they are 240 days old, too late for the credit division president to take action to change operating income for the positive. Keleghan could only increase reserves for delinquencies that would have had a negative effect on operating income. It was far too late to change the existing mix of cardholders. Keleghan's only possible response option was antithetical to the company's goals—a powerful incentive for anyone in that position to conceal information, as Lacy alleged.[22] The credit division president would need real-time information on leading economic indicators that might suggest an economic downturn that would lead to increasing delinquencies more than 240 days in the future. Only then would he or she have response options that permitted changing credit approval policies. Let's not kid ourselves—the cost of developing real-time information flows (even if one knew what the nine-month leading indicators of the economy were) would be prohibitive. However, if this information on one of the most critical business processes had been reported more widely at Sears, these data could have provided an adequate event–impact lag (table 4-4).

Although the head of the credit business did not have appropriate response options, the CEO has many more response options available to him as a result of real-time information on delinquencies. Some of the response options are clearly delineated in the steps taken after the announcement of the surprise increase in reserves. Due to the decrease in profitability, Lacy noted that, while the credit business expected a quick return to

TABLE 4-4

Identification Model for Sears

Highest-priority goal	Credit division revenues
Causal events	Cards issued, balances carried, delinquencies, state of economy
Metric	Percentage of delinquencies, consumer debt (entire economy)
Response options available	Greater focus on growth and revenue of other divisions; increasing reserves for uncollectable accounts

stability, the company would slow investments in store redesign and slow the deployment of Lands' End merchandise to some store locations. Sears would count on cost controls to compensate for depressed credit earnings.[23] Lacy also discussed some efforts at accelerating merchandise growth plans. Of course, there were also plans for strengthening the credit portfolio. Any and all of these responses could have been undertaken well before October and minimized the profitability hit the company took in the third quarter. Additionally, a more gradual increase in reserves spread over several quarters would also have reduced the impact of the surprise—a $3.4 billion drop in market capitalization in one day.

Sears ultimately decided that the damage caused by inadequate monitoring and reporting on the credit portfolio had surprised the company too many times. In the spring of 2003, Sears announced that its credit business was for sale, and it announced in July 2003 that it had concluded a deal to sell its $29 billion in receivables to Citigroup for $3 billion.[24]

Ending Suspected Events

Suspected events, as mentioned in chapter 1, are the most maddening of surprises—the data to stop the surprise were there; they were just not in the right hands. The Sears and Boeing stories illustrate the critical role real-time reporting plays in ending these types of surprises. Certainly these stories should lead every manager to seek information that already exists in their organization that may give them a heads-up about an approaching disaster or opportunity that would otherwise be a surprise. As both examples illustrate as well, information sharing is crucial to successful real-time opportunity detection. The Sears story particularly foreshadows some of the issues that must be confronted as real-time opportunity detection is deployed across an enterprise. In the quest to end surprises not just for individual managers but for the corporation as a whole, traditional silos of information must be broken down and real-time data shared, concepts that we'll examine more in chapters 6 and 7 as we look at the process of moving from limited deployments of real-time opportunity detection to becoming a real-time enterprise.

5

surmounted events:
getting it right

Surmounted event: The event is reported in time and effective action is taken.

MANY FREQUENT BUSINESS TRAVELERS can recite the Federal Aviation Administration's prescribed safety speech from memory. While it is intuitively clear why we must put on our seatbelts, raise our tray tables, and return our seats to their full upright position as the airplane prepares to land, the admonition to turn off all electronic devices prior to landing is more opaque. Plenty of business travelers have ignored the warning, concealed their Palm Pilot or laptop as much as possible, and kept working, hoping to eke out a few more minutes of productivity before arrival. If more travelers knew the reason for the rule, compliance with the request would certainly be far more rapid and comprehensive.

You see, an incredibly complex real-time system kicks in as planes approach for landing—and since this system could save the lives of everyone aboard, the FAA has determined that even the slightest risk of interference is unacceptable. The system, known as the instrument landing system (ILS), is a ground-based radio operating system that broadcasts the aircraft's position, course, altitude, and other critical flight data to corresponding receivers located on the aircraft to help pilots navigate regardless of visibility conditions.[1] Obviously this system is most critical in low-visibility situations when pilots often engage "autoland" computers to use the information being transmitted from the ground to land the airplane without pilot intervention.[2] In these situations, the ILS broadcasts are monitored, captured, and analyzed by the autoland computers aboard the aircraft that can respond by completely controlling all flight and navigation functions. Thus, in dangerous low-visibility situations, a potential suspected event regularly becomes a surmounted event when the plane lands successfully, all without the knowledge of the passengers who are wondering why they cannot listen to their CD players. In the wake of the terrorists attacks on September 11, 2001, these real-time autoland systems may be enhanced even further to allow aircraft to be flown and landed by remote control.[3]

In many ways, it is difficult to understand why real-time surveillance, like that aboard airplanes, of critical day-to-day business events is not more readily incorporated into the daily regimen of employees, managers, executives, and even board directors. After all, the notion of monitoring, capturing, analyzing, reporting, and responding to critical information is not an alien concept in our day-to-day activities.

- We depend on real-time information about the time of day to make it to meetings on time.

- We rely on thermostats in our homes and office buildings to respond instantly with more heat or air conditioning when the temperature rises or drops beyond a certain point.

- We expect the gauges in our cars to reflect real-time information on our speed (especially when we see a semi-concealed police car) and fuel status.

- We watch the meter at the self-service gas pump to make certain we stop the flow of gas when we reach the desired amount.

- We use smoke and fire detectors to warn us immediately of danger, especially while we are asleep.

- We even use temperature-sensitive pop-up buttons to tell us when to take a Thanksgiving turkey out of the oven.

We are surrounded by examples of real-time monitoring, capturing, analyzing, reporting, and responding to events. Despite the damage caused by business surprises attributable to an absence of real-time information and the prevalence of real-time information in our personal lives, little is being done to change the business culture and processes that tolerate surprises and to begin using real-time opportunity detection. However, as Alan Greenspan, chairman of the Federal Reserve, noted in a speech in August 2002, the use of real-time information is slowly but surely beginning to have an impact: "Economic imbalances in recent years apparently have been addressed more expeditiously and effectively than in the past, aided importantly by the more widespread availability and intensive use of real-time information."[4]

In certain companies all across the economy, managers are predicting the present, detecting opportunities in real time, and what were once surprise events or suspected events are becoming surmounted events.

Amberwood Homes

Surprises are a way of life in the construction industry. While not as complex as assembling commercial aircraft, a precise sequence of events must be followed. Electrical work has to be done before insulation is installed; both require inspection before drywall can be put up; roofs must be watertight before any of these steps can be completed. Any unanticipated deviations in the specific schedule can add weeks and months to a project as one subcontractor arrives at a job, encounters a surprise event and determines that nothing can be done because some prior step has not yet been completed as anticipated and moves on to other jobs. As anyone who's been involved in building a new house or remodeling an existing one can tell you, the biggest surprise is when the project is actually completed on time. While schedule problems are a major irritant to a homeowner, they are even more costly to the builders. Subcontractors charge a fee to show up at a job site regardless of whether they can complete their task or not. A builder also incurs fees for schedule overruns because the length of time a project must be financed increases.

Amberwood Homes, a large custom home builder in Arizona, one of the nation's hottest (literally and figuratively) construction markets, has made some significant changes to processes and culture to eliminate scheduling surprises. Over the years, each construction superintendent at Amberwood had developed his or her own process for tracking progress on a house and setting subcontractor schedules. In fact, according to Dan Johnson, construction manager at Amberwood, many of the subcontractors did not maintain schedules at all.[5] Johnson saw the opportunity to significantly improve operations by centralizing progress reports and making real-time adjustments to schedules. Today, each of Amberwood's superintendents and more than fifty subcontractors use a new real-time scheduling system to ensure that no unnecessary trips are made and everyone on a job knows what the current status is at each house under construction—typically twenty to twenty-five at any given time. Superintendents use wireless devices to update progress on a job site as each step of the process is completed. A new schedule is generated as adjustments are made. Each morning subcontractors check the schedule to ensure that they are going to the right houses at the right time.

The impetus for putting the new process in place was the critical nature of controlling expenses in the construction industry, where net margins average around 5 percent. Mike Farrar, vice president of marketing, says that at Amberwood, "cost management is king." Johnson estimates that the new focus on real-time schedules has cut the time to complete a house from six months to five months. Cutting time to completion by thirty days saves $3,000 to $4,000 per project in finance charges. The savings from finance charges alone may amount to a 20 percent boost in margin.[6] The savings also dramatically affect the availability of working capital to invest in new houses, which enables Amberwood to grow faster than it has in the past. Another benefit to Amberwood has been the reduction in administrative costs related to fees—both fees the subcontractors charge Amberwood when they arrive at a job site to find that they cannot work because a prior task hasn't been completed and fees Amberwood charges subcontractors when they do not show up on schedule. In the past, foreman and managers had to spend time sorting out and debating the validity of these charges, which kept foremen out of the field where they are most valuable. The new system eliminates all Amberwood's charges (for scheduling a crew that was not needed) and makes any penalties assessed on the subcontractors easy to verify. In fact, Johnson says that the data have allowed Amberwood to more effectively make decisions on hiring or firing subcontractor firms. Without the real-time system, assessment of a particular subcontractor would be based on the "gut feel" of foremen about performance. The real-time scheduling system allows Amberwood to evaluate subcontractors against each other and over time.

Amberwood perceives additional "soft" improvements to its business from the real-time schedule. As the company's ability to deliver houses to customers without any surprises in the schedule has grown, there has been a noticeable up-tick in customer satisfaction rates. Amberwood considers this response crucial because roughly 40 percent of the business comes from referrals from past customers. Recently Amberwood has also made the real-time schedule updates directly available to its customers via Amberwood's Web site. Mike Farrar says that the company immediately noticed an improvement in its competitive position for customers who are relocating to Phoenix: "These customers are moving to Arizona from all over the country, and they account for 30 to 35 percent of our customers. They can check on the progress of their new home from wherever they are and it helps them plan their relocation schedule and avoid having to find temporary housing like others have had to in the past when a project was delayed without their knowledge and they arrived in Phoenix to find their house wouldn't be ready for another month. They consider the real-time schedule a big plus in choosing to build with us."

The Amberwood experience points to a particularly important point in developing real-time processes. While technology is a significant enabler ("The wireless updates to a central database take a lot of errors and often hours of phone calls out of the process," says Johnson), the real challenge for Johnson was getting everyone involved to change their way of thinking. "Most of our subcontractors have been doing these jobs for years and they have always done things the same way. Any change takes time. Getting them to adopt this new real-time way of scheduling and managing projects was similar to a framer adjusting from wood framing to steel framing. It takes time and effort."

Johnson noted that there are still some subcontractors who have not adjusted to the new system: "They still think they can

TABLE 5-1

Identification and Justification Models for Amberwood

Identification

Highest-priority goal	Construction cost management
Causal events	Subcontractor work schedules
Metric	Tasks completed
Response options available	Updating schedule to maximize personnel usage and eliminate delays and trip charges due to inaccurate schedules

Justification

Alignment with corporate mission/vision	Yes (quality construction, customer satisfaction).
Alignment with priorities	Yes (cost management, maximization of working capital).
Materiality	Resources are reallocated when warranted by schedule changes.
Corporate impact	Savings of $3,000 to $4,000 per house; estimated 10 to 20 percent improvement in net margins.

just call a foreman in the morning and tell him that they're not coming." The majority adapted after just a few months, however. "Everyone began to see the benefits," says Johnson. "It's not just Amberwood that saves money, but the subs save money too because they can see a schedule months ahead of time, which allows them to better plan inventory purchasing and staff more efficiently. In fact, when we began sending the subcontractor companies weekly and monthly reports on their performance, many of the owners called to tell us that our reports gave them more insight into their business than they had ever had before." Amberwood's adoption of real-time opportunity detection allows all the involved parties to increase productivity and save time and money (table 5-1).

Wet Seal, Inc.

Tight margins in the construction industry drive an intense focus on cost management. In the retail industry margins are equally tight, but the emphasis is on inventory management. Success or failure is often measured by no more than having the right products in the right store at the right time. Selling out of a product means lost revenue, often with no chance to recover. By the time inventories can be restocked, most customers will have found the item elsewhere. Protecting against inventory shortfalls by overstocking leads to significant margin erosion as the goods left over have to be marked down or shipped to an overstock dealer. Wal-Mart Stores' use of technology for efficient inventory management has set benchmarks for every industry and has put particular pressure on every company in the retail business, whether it is a direct competitor of Wal-Mart or not.

Wet Seal, Inc., is a mall-based clothing retailer with over six hundred stores (operating under the Wet Seal, Arden B, and Zutopia brands) and more than $600 million in revenue in 2002. Chief information officer Michael Relich was brought on with the specific mission to use technology to improve inventory management. He states the problem this way: "The chief impediment was that each store was an island; there was no reliable way of getting information from the stores to district and regional managers so they could properly manage inventory."[7] Store managers created weekly sales updates by hand and phoned or faxed them to district managers who were compiling the reports on yellow legal pads, according to Ron Hunt, operations manager at Wet Seal.

Perceiving the need to enable regional and district managers to distribute inventory more efficiently, Relich installed new point-of-sale systems with a DSL line in each store to connect to headquarters via a virtual private network.[8] "Each night we get a full report from all six hundred plus stores on everything that was sold that day," he explains. When the district and regional managers come into the office each morning, they find a report waiting in their e-mail inboxes that aggregates all the information from all the stores in their area. They can then instantly reallocate inventory based on which stores need what products.

TABLE 5-2

Identification and Justification Models for Wet Seal

Identification

Highest-priority goal	Effective allocation of inventory
Causal events	Store sales to identify trends in buying and shortages of inventory
Metric	Raw sales of each item
Response options available	Allocate inventory to maximize sales growth and reduce markdowns

Justification

Alignment with corporate mission/vision	Yes. ("[We succeed] by giving teenage girls, America's most fickle buyers, exactly what they want, when they want!" —From corporate history)
Alignment with priorities	Yes. (Inventory management is key success factor in retail.)
Materiality	District and regional managers allocate inventory based on real-time sales data.
Corporate impact	Growing same-store sales and reduced markdowns to clear inventory.

"Moving inventory fast is especially important for us because our core market is very trend-conscious women. If you lose a customer because you're out of inventory on a hot item, you not only lose that sale, you lose some mindshare. There's no guarantee that person will come back to the store for the next hot trend item," says Relich.

Additionally, the real-time information on sales at individual stores allows district managers to find problems quickly. If same-store sales are lagging or one store in a district isn't keeping up with others, the managers are able to identify the problem early and focus their attention on resolving it quickly (table 5-2). The real-time information is also helping resolve another pressing problem in the retail industry, *shrinkage*, more popularly known as shoplifting. "Our next goal is to more closely connect sales, expected and actual inventory to quickly identify stores that are having the biggest problems with shrinkage," says Relich. "Shrinkage drives the managers crazy. Once a problem is identified managers can immediately go check out the stores in person to look for holes in security and get them closed."

Ford Motor Company

Both Amberwood and Wet Seal have begun real-time opportunity detection under favorable market conditions. In the overall malaise of the economy since 2001, the few bright spots have been in consumer spending and the housing market, both of which have continued to grow. The construction industry in particular is enjoying the best housing market since the 1950s and perhaps ever in history; Amberwood is capitalizing on the growth by improving the most important line item in its business, construction expenses. Meanwhile, there is another industry where cost management has become critical because the market news has not been nearly so positive. Although 2002 saw new records in both new car and new home sales, in the home industry prices were appreciating rapidly while in the automotive industry real prices were falling. Driven by large cash needs (we'll examine the genesis of this need and how General Motors is transforming its whole enterprise in response to it in the next chapter), most manufacturers needed to keep car sales volumes strong. As a result, unprecedented cash rebates and 0 percent financing offers became commonplace. This in turn slashed profit margins and has raised cost management to the top priority at Ford Motor.

The need for extreme focus on cost management at Ford is an outgrowth of its success in the late 1990s when the company was the most profitable manufacturer in the United States. During this time Ford's costs for parts and production grew faster than those of its competition. The impact was not immediately obvious as Ford enjoyed blockbuster profits on its trucks and SUVs. As profits eroded, however, the scope of the problems at Ford came into sharper focus. The board replaced CEO Jacques Nasser with William Clay Ford Jr. in late 2001 in an effort to start a turnaround at the company that was now the highest-cost large auto maker in the world. In early 2002, Ford announced its turnaround plan—a plan that includes closing five plants (all in North America), cutting shifts and jobs at thirteen others, and laying off 35,000 workers. The goal is to save $9 billion by the middle of the decade. One of the most critical parts of the plan, the key to long-term competitiveness, calls for a $700 reduction in the cost of producing each car by 2005, resulting in total savings of more than $3 billion; $200 of that reduction was to happen by the end of 2002.

However, in July 2002, less than six months into the plan, CFO Allan Gilmour announced that the cost-cutting plan was behind schedule. With this early warning, five months before the target was to be reached, executives had response options that would not have been available two or three months later. If this shortfall had not been reported until October or November, Ford executives would have been forced to acknowledge failure or cut more jobs to meet targets. With six more months before the targets needed to be reached, executives were able to devise a response that did not involve cutting more jobs and closing more plants than had already been scheduled. In fact, rather than cutting more jobs, Ford decided to add seven hundred new cost-engineering jobs, more than tripling the existing three hundred. These engineers were charged with reviewing each major component (for example, drivetrain, brakes, frame) of every model to find ways to save money on production. For instance, the engineers determined that frame reinforcements in Ford Explorers could be redesigned to provide the same level of safety while costing $100 less per vehicle.

Executives realized that it would take more than just additional staff focused on cutting costs to meet goals, however. The three senior executives in charge of overseeing vehicle production cost-management efforts—Phil Martens, vice president for vehicle programs, David Thursfield, head of global purchasing and international operations, and James Padilla, group vice president for North America—decreed that each engineer had to deliver a daily report on the status of their projects. The three executives review these reports each night to gauge progress toward the company's overall goals. The daily reports have had a dramatic impact: by September, just two months after Gilmour's warning, chief operating officer Nick Scheele was announcing that the company would exceed 2002's $200 goal by 20 percent, which would save Ford an additional $150 million or more. One of the ways this rapid increase in the rate of progress was accomplished was by allowing executives to see where their efforts were most needed. For instance, according to the *Wall Street Journal,* Thursfield, realizing that cost cutting in radios was not sufficient, met with senior executives of Visteon, Ford's radio supplier, to hammer out a plan to further reduce costs by $220 million.[9]

It's worth noting that uniquely among the examples of surmounted events, Ford's efforts did not require the use of technology beyond e-mail. Ford's real-time opportunity detection efforts have been based, thus far, entirely on changing the process by which progress in cost cutting is measured and reported. While technology may at some point improve this process further, Ford highlights the fact that technology is only a secondary consideration in achieving gains via predicting the present. Far more important is the change in management thinking about monitoring crucial data in real time (see table 5-3).

Ford's revitalization plan has many hurdles ahead of it and success is far from assured. However, meeting the key goal of

TABLE 5-3

Identification and Justification Models for Ford

Identification

Highest-priority goal	Cut cost of vehicle production
Causal events	Cost engineers' review of major automobile systems
Metric	Daily progress toward reaching $200 savings per vehicle by year end 2002
Response options available	Increase focus on certain vehicles or systems; increase executive attention to suppliers

Justification

Alignment with corporate mission/vision	Yes. ("Our vision is to become the world's leading consumer company for automotive products and services"; cost management essential to gaining market share.)
Alignment with priorities	Yes. (See numerous statements by Bill Ford about critical importance of reducing vehicle production costs rapidly.)
Materiality	Padilla, Thursfield, and Martens become involved in delayed cost-saving projects.
Corporate impact	30 percent of $9 billion in committed savings to come from cutting vehicle production costs.

the plan, reducing vehicle production costs, is now far more likely to happen. If the plan stays ahead of schedule as a result of the focus on daily reports, Ford might have the room it needs to adjust other parts of the plan if and when difficulties are encountered (for instance, in negotiating labor reduction plans with the United Auto Workers and other unions).

Dresdner Kleinwort Wasserstein

Real-time disciplines are not being applied just in material goods industries. Service industries are also beginning to catch on to the benefits of real-time opportunity detection. The financial services industry, from stock markets to ATMs, has depended on real-time information for decades. More recently, though, the use of real-time information is spreading inside financial services firms. One example is Dresdner Kleinwort Wasserstein.[10]

The banking crises of the early twentieth century led law-makers to heavily regulate banks and associated financial services firms. The express intent of these regulations was to limit the risk to individuals of banks failing and taking consumers' life savings with them. Of course, limiting individuals' risk meant limiting banks' exposure to market risks. For instance, banks were prevented from dealing in insurance (and insurance com-panies were prevented from providing banking services) or ex-posing themselves too heavily to stock markets.

In the latter half of the twentieth century, however, liberal economic theories prevailed, and governments around the world began allowing the free market to determine interest rates and currency exchange rates. At the same time, deregulation of the financial services industry accelerated.[11] As a result, financial services firms have an ever-widening array of new and highly complex investment instruments. Key among these new invest-ment instruments are so-called derivative products, such as op-tions, interest rate swaps, and futures.[12] As these and other similarly complex products have become more accepted and without the protection of highly regulated currency exchange and interest rates, the risk assumed by financial institutions has grown rapidly and therefore the need for risk management has increased dramatically.

The danger involved with derivatives and the need for risk management was made abundantly clear in 1995 after a lone rogue trader in the Singapore office of a 223-year-old bank known as Barings PLC caused the firm to fall into bankruptcy. The agent of Barings's demise, Nicholas Leeson, traded in fu-tures and options: He had hoped to buy products at a low price on one exchange and create a profit by selling the same product for a higher price on another exchange. By February 1995, losses from Leeson's unauthorized trades totaled approximately $1.2 billion.[13] The key factor in Leeson's actions was his ability to purposefully keep his exposure to various investment instru-ments secret from bank management, highlighting a larger issue that many banks faced as they expanded globally. With volatility higher, risk greater, and hundreds of traders operating all over the world, it was nearly impossible for a financial services firm to understand its global exposure given certain market changes. This ignorance led to a number of situations where investment decisions were made that overexposed a bank to a particular currency or interest rate or where a risk was hedged too much and returns were damaged.

The new banking laws, updated securities regulations, added complexities of new financial instruments such as derivatives, and the Barings bankruptcy all served as a backdrop in the late 1990s when executives at Dresdner Kleinwort Wasserstein decided to build a real-time risk management system. The goal of the risk management system was to "obtain a real-time, consistent view of risk and capital utilization on a global basis."[14]

The system uses complex calculations to determine the bank's level of exposure to any particular market condition and to compare it to a pre-established risk tolerance level. Dresdner began with its equities operations and proceeded slowly because of the large number of trading systems, both externally purchased and developed in house, that were in use throughout the firm. Executives understood that while there were major risk management benefits that could be achieved by having a global real time view of exposure, the daily operations of traders and managers could not be impeded at all.

Of course, the need at Dresdner—at any bank for that matter—was not just to understand all the positions it held globally at any point in time but to correlate that information with real-time information on market changes around the world. To achieve these objectives, Dresdner negotiated to obtain real-time information from third-party market data providers such as Reuters to immediately capture and depict changes in market conditions, movements in prices, changes in interest rates, and a host of other external factors that could increase or decrease the value of securities. This real-time information was then integrated into Dresdner's systems to update the firm's risk assessment conclusions and transmit recommended changes to system users in Dresdner offices around the world. Additionally, automated alerting systems would advise users whenever a predetermined threshold of change had been reached. As a result, Dresdner can now manage trading strategies across the globe in different products and derivatives and most important, can maximize its returns on capital. The system gives the bank a timely and consistent global view of risk, with the ability to see position, profit and loss, and market sensitivity with a four-minute delay (or less) around the world. Dresdner has come to rely on the system so much that one official estimated that they could potentially lose millions of dollars if the risk management system lost its real-time feed on market conditions for just one hour.

Just as was the case at Amberwood, the benefits of the real-time risk management system go beyond the initial goals. The process of creating the system also improved other parts of Dresdner's operations:

1. Data quality has improved, accompanied by reduced costs for exception handling and improvement in back-office processing throughput. The improvement has occurred because errors (such as in pricing) often show up as an unexpected change in exposure. Because these changes are seen in nearly real time, corrections can be made in the source systems before the error is propagated to multiple back-office systems. This has reduced the number of end-of-day exceptions to a level considered marginal.

2. Daily reports—such as the global scenario reports Dresdner uses to ensure that executives are aware of global market changes—are now available first thing next morning instead of two days later because of the availability of consistent, high-quality data.

3. The process of implementing the system required rationalization of both existing systems and data, including eliminating or consolidating redundant reporting systems and market reference data feeds. This has led to reduced costs and personnel requirements.

4. Time to market for new initiatives and products has improved because of reduced complexity and inconsistencies. Dresdner anticipates that the system will soon allow

real time in the real world

TABLE 5-4

Identification and Justification Models for Dresdner Kleinwort Wasserstein

Identification

Highest-priority goal	Risk management
Causal events	Current positions held by the various global offices of Dresdner; changes in interest rates, currency, and other news events
Metric	Real-time risk threshold
Response options available	Direct proper trades to increase, decrease, or hedge certain holdings

Justification

Alignment with corporate mission/vision	Yes. ("Allianz stands for profitable growth"; profitability is impossible without proper risk management.)
Alignment with priorities	Yes. ("Optimizing the economic value added of our group, based on risk-adequate capital requirements and sustainable growth targets; exploiting high-growth market opportunities by leveraging our traditional risk management expertise.")
Materiality	Changes in market conditions that tip risk out of balance are immediately reported to managers for action.
Corporate impact	Potential millions of dollars of losses from interruption of real-time information for just an hour.

it to improve regulatory reporting and client statement delivery as well.

5. In addition to risk management employees, the system is used by operations and trader support functions to check position and trade bookings and by data administrators to check for missing reference data that could affect trade settlement.

At the end of the day, however, the most critical benefit for Dresdner is the ability to engage in intraday decision making on an enterprisewide basis with confidence in the supporting data (see table 5-4).[15]

eBay

At Dresdner, the need for risk management in real time grew from a desire to improve the organization's core competency and generate short-term profitability. Another services firm, eBay, took on real-time opportunity detection to shore up an area that was not a core competency but could have a dramatic impact on long-term revenues.

The role of a corporate mission statement is to articulate the purpose of an organization and therefore explain why that organization exists.[16] The award for shortest and clearest mission statement could easily go to eBay: "eBay's mission is to help practically anyone trade practically anything on earth."[17] (See Identification and Justification Models for eBay in table 5-5.)

From time to time, however, some eBay users have tested the boundaries of what "practically anything" really means, resulting in the close scrutiny of the company and its policies by

TABLE 5-5

Identification and Justification Models for eBay

Identification

Highest-priority goal	Removing impediments to growing user base
Causal events	Offensive listings, breaking news stories
Metric	Listings related to news stories
Response options available	Removal of offensive listings before they are exposed to the eBay community

Justification

Alignment with corporate mission/vision	Yes. ("To help practically anyone trade practically anything on earth"; helping more people requires creating a safe and trusted environment for users.)
Alignment with priorities	Yes. (eBay states that revenue growth is highly dependent on "community cohesion and interaction.")
Materiality	Offensive listings are removed; if doubt exists, decision is escalated to senior executive.
Corporate impact	Potential damage to reputation and long-term growth prospects.

both the press and the public. The attention-grabbing examples became so rampant for a time that an organization named :n/e/tsurf established a Web site to list the individual cases that tested the boundaries. Following are some examples:

- A teenager put his soul up for auction.

- A man put himself up for auction to find a date for Valentine's Day.

- A person who was never identified offered five hundred pounds of marijuana.

- A protestor against government corruption offered his vote in Maryland elections for auction in a satirical display.

In general, these "items" are somewhat amusing, but eBay has had to deal with far more serious issues than these—items that many have found deeply offensive. The items that caused the largest issue for the longest time were items significant to hate groups, such as Nazi memorabilia, but problems were not isolated to swastikas and Ku Klux Klan banners. In one instance, a death row inmate tried to sell five seats to his execution. For a time there were frequent offers of human remains (one listing was for a "Real Human Skull from the Korean War") and human organs. A man dying of AIDS listed his body, and someone tried to auction three unborn children.[18]

eBay executives knew from the beginning of their venture that buyers' trust in the system was critical to success and that a major challenge therefore would be dealing with sellers attempting to defraud buyers on the site. As the site rapidly grew and offensive items began appearing with more regularity, eBay executives quickly realized the harm that could be inflicted on its reputation and its ability to attract and keep customers and investors if they did not also address the placement of offensive material on its site. As a result, eBay executives responded with changes to auctioning policies whenever a major new category of unsavory items appeared on its site.[19]

Although attempts to auction offensive items such as hate material and human organs were being addressed by eBay executives through changes in policies, it was more difficult for eBay to respond to questionable items offered for auction that were inspired by sudden events in the news:

1. Soon after six-year-old Elian Gonzalez survived his voyage from Cuba to Florida in 1999, the raft that Elian and others supposedly clung to as they approached the United States was listed.[20]

2. Immediately after Oklahoma City bomber Timothy McVeigh's execution, someone attempted to sell his death certificate as well as copies of his last statement.[21]

3. In the wake of the 2000 presidential election controversy in Florida, two men placed a stolen Palm Beach County voting machine on the site.[22]

4. Minutes after golfer Payne Stewart's plane crashed into a South Dakota field in October 1999, killing everyone aboard, adoring fans and macabre collectors started bidding up prices for the pro's memorabilia.[23]

In each case, eBay executives were faced with a quandary. The best way to grow eBay's revenues was to increase the number of auctions. The best way to increase the number of auctions was to attract more and more potential buyers. Taking a long-term view, executives realized that while boosting site visits in the short term, these sensational offerings would damage the reputation and public standing of the company. Just like the supermarket that drives away its best customers by allowing bad produce to remain on display beside fresh greens, eBay would lose potential buyers who associated the site with the grotesque and the macabre rather than high-quality items.

Chief operating officer Maynard Webb and his management team came to the conclusion that only by supplementing eBay's efforts to keep its listing policies up to date with real-time detection of inappropriate items related to breaking news could the company stave off potential damage to its long-term prospects. As a result, eBay was able to turn the aftermath of September 11, 2001, into a surmounted event.

The timeline of that day began before 7:00 A.M. as terrorists boarded four planes bound for the West Coast. The first plane struck the North Tower of the World Trade Center at 8:45 A.M., but most people did not realize the nature of what was happening until the second plane struck the South Tower at 9:03 A.M. The shock and horror deepened when the South Tower collapsed at 10:05 A.M. Twenty-three minutes later the North Tower collapsed. Within five minutes the first of several listings was entered on eBay's site offering rubble from the World Trade Center.

Although it is almost certain that the listings were fraudulent, the impact of the public revulsion for such crass profiteering would have reflected negatively on eBay. But eBay's reputation remains unscathed. Why? Because, although many of us heard that rubble was listed, we also heard that "someone *tried* to auction rubble from the World Trade Center." The word "tried" makes all the difference—we view the individuals who made the attempt to sell rubble with distaste but view eBay with trust because it acted quickly to remove the items within minutes of the listings becoming available to the general eBay user via its search engine.

What Went Right?

How did eBay find the rubble so quickly among the tens of thousands of items listed on the site? By using real-time information, but not real-time information about the listings. Listings come in so fast that it would require a vast staff to monitor all of them, significantly dampening eBay's profits. Maynard Webb and his team realized that monitoring all the auctions was impossible logistically, but that to protect eBay's brand image, offensive material had to be found quickly. While eBay has a large group of loyal users who notify the company of perceived abuse (for example, fraudulent listings and bids and offensive material), Webb felt that the company needed to project an image of being proactive rather than reactive in these situations. In 1999, he realized that the antecedent events that needed monitoring would be in news reports. By watching real-time news sources, a select group of individuals (whom eBay colloquially calls "watchers") could predict the present and watch for specific listings inspired by breaking news. By monitoring the news in real time, an effective response—removal of certain listings—could happen before much of eBay's community was exposed to the material.

The "watchers" have the task of searching for and intercepting attempts to place offensive material on the auction site. To accomplish their objectives, they consistently monitor the news for stories that might inspire sellers to offer for sale objectionable items related to the story in question. By comparing new items placed for auction in eBay's search engine with factors involved in a given news story, the "watchers" are able to quickly identify and challenge questionable items for sale. When an item's suitability is unclear, the "watchers" follow a preestablished escalation procedure to obtain a real-time ruling on whether the item in question should be withdrawn from the site. On the morning of September 11, Webb had to make the call (CEO Meg Whitman was traveling in Asia at the time). He decided that rubble would be removed but that World Trade Center souvenirs such as posters, snow globes, and models would remain on the site.

eBay's real-time monitoring of news events was tested once again early in 2003 when the Space Shuttle *Columbia* broke up over Texas as it returned home. On February 1 at 9:00 A.M. EST, NASA's mission control in Houston lost voice and data telemetry contact with *Columbia*. During this time some residents of Texas heard a loud explosion and saw a high-flying vehicle streaking across the sky. At 9:31, NASA announced that search-and-rescue efforts were being initiated in response to the apparent catastrophic destruction of the shuttle *Columbia*.[24] By 10:54, just one hour and fifty-four minutes after contact with the space shuttle had abruptly ended, "Space Shuttle *Columbia* debris" was put up for auction on eBay. A normal delay took place at eBay between 10:54 and the point when the next refresh of items for sale took place (refreshes occur every one to four hours). At 12:15 P.M. the *Columbia* debris auction was discovered and removed from the eBay site. Shortly after this incident, five other similar auctions were placed on eBay and removed minutes after becoming accessible to the general public.[25]

Conclusion

The practices of the five companies discussed in this chapter provide clear evidence of the business benefits of ending surprises and capitalizing on real-time information. The companies rely on technology to differing degrees to accomplish real-time opportunity detection, but all are focusing on a limited range of information about the present to ensure that surprises are avoided and opportunities are exploited. Each of these organizations as well is applying real-time information and the principles of real-time opportunity detection to only a limited part of their business. Wet Seal is not tracking all its purchasing in real time; Ford is only beginning to consider tracking real-time sales information. Although they are enjoying the results of their current real-time efforts, none of these companies is yet a real-time enterprise. Part 3 looks at the steps necessary to expand real-time opportunity detection across the enterprise and the business benefits that go along with taking those steps.

from real-time opportunity detection to real-time enterprise

IF YOU WERE TO EXAMINE an aerial view of any factory constructed in the 1800s, you would notice that it resembles the shape of the letter *T*. The reason for this design was that machines were powered by a water wheel, and later by steam-powered engines. The wheel or engine resided at the top of the T and drove a long drive shaft that traversed the entire length of the building (figure P-3). A belt connected each machine to the drive shaft. When the common drive shaft turned, all the belts moved and powered the machines.

According to Stanford economics professor Paul A. David, when independent electrical motors replaced the common drive shaft system, expectations for productivity gains were not realized. In fact, Professor David's research shows that it took another forty years before significant gains in productivity occurred.[1] One of the key reasons for the delay in achieving productivity gains was that factory managers kept their machines exactly where they were when they were powered

FIGURE P-3

An "aerial" view of a typical nineteenth-century steam-powered factory shows how machines in the factory had to be configured.

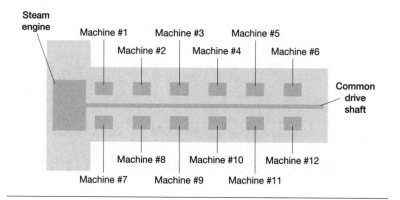

by steam, rather than reorganizing the machines' locations to gain greater efficiencies.

Real-time opportunity detection, as applied by Ford, eBay, and others, provides real opportunities for success. However, just as the factories of the 1800s needed real change to achieve substantial productivity gains, organizations must deploy real change if they are to achieve the maximum benefits of real-time opportunity detection. Although limited deployments of real-time information and real-time opportunity detection are certainly beneficial, truly transformational benefits from real-time information come only from implementing real-time opportunity detection in all the most critical operations of a business. To apply widespread real-time opportunity detection, companies must review policies, practices, and procedures on corporate governance, risk management, corporate liability, and a host of other issues and be willing to change any or all of them.

Part 3 identifies some of the changes likely to occur as companies spread real-time opportunity detection throughout the most critical business processes and equip themselves, via process and management changes, to become Real-Time Enterprises. Chapter 6 looks at the steps required to move from limited, single-point implementations of real-time opportunity detection to becoming true Real-Time Enterprises. Chapter 7 looks at the new corporate roles and responsibilities required to successfully make the transition to Real-Time Enterprises. Finally, chapter 8 looks at how real-time opportunity detection and Real-Time Enterprises will evolve over the next ten to fifteen years and the inevitable changes in industries and economies that will result.

6

following through: deploying real-time opportunity detection across the enterprise

A Real-Time Enterprise (RTE) both engages in real-time opportunity detection in all its critical business processes and further improves its performance by redesigning all processes needed to improve its ability to respond to events efficiently and effectively when required.

AMBERWOOD, DRESDNER, Wet Seal, Ford, and eBay are all doing a remarkable job of real-time opportunity detection. They have identified areas of their business where capturing real-time information and delivering it to the right managers can have an immediate impact in improving business results. Despite this early success, they still have a long way to go to reach the ultimate goal—ending all business surprises by being real-time enterprises. The initial deployment of real-time opportunity detection is just the first of three steps on the road to becoming a real-time enterprise. Real-time enterprises both move the detection of any event that affects their most critical business processes into real time and improve their ability to respond to these events when they occur.

Becoming a Real-Time Enterprise

Becoming a Real-Time Enterprise involves three steps:

- *Step 1:* Begin real-time opportunity detection.

- *Step 2:* Deploy real-time opportunity detection across the enterprise.

- *Step 3:* Overhaul processes to improve the organization's ability to respond.

Although the three steps to becoming a real-time enterprise are logically distinct and appear linear, in practice the lines between the steps are not nearly so clear. Steps 1 and 2 can be combined by immediately looking at real-time opportunity detection from the corporate perspective. Steps 2 and 3 can be taken simultaneously—in fact, it will be necessary for many companies to do so as processes are redesigned to generate real-time information so that real-time opportunity detection can be implemented.

Part 2 was dedicated to step 1. It looked at companies that could have benefited from taking the first step, as well as five companies that have taken it: In some significant part of their business they have begun capturing, monitoring, and reporting vital real-time information. In this chapter we look at steps 2 and 3.

Step 2: Deploy Real-Time Opportunity Detection Across the Enterprise

In the second step, executives and managers spread real-time opportunity detection throughout the enterprise so that all critical business processes and functions are being monitored in real time. In chapter 2, we looked at the process of determining what real-time information to monitor from the perspective of the individual manager. When taking the next step—to deploy real-time opportunity detection to the entire enterprise (driven by senior executives rather than individual managers) so that all the corporation's most critical business processes are being mon-

For organizations with an implemented and well-documented corporate-level operations management framework (for example, BSC or EFQM), another approach is possible to focus corporate energies in deploying real-time opportunity detection across the enterprise. Given that these management frameworks have already identified the goals and priorities of the organization as a whole, executives can simply plug these metrics directly into the Identification and Justification Models to determine which metrics merit real-time monitoring. Using these metrics provides a simple shortcut to identify corporate level goals and priorities.

An added benefit of taking this approach is that it can serve as an objective check on how the performance management framework has been implemented across the company. Implementation guides for the various frameworks dictate that each manager's goals should be directly related to the corporate metrics. When evaluating the corporate metrics in the Identification Model, it is not unusual to find that many of them do not provide event–impact lags large enough for appropriate responses. Following the Identification Model's prescribed path to identify causal events is necessary; in doing so executives have a useful check on the way the management framework has been deployed. If the causal events for one of the corporate performance metrics are not reflected in the versions of the performance framework of individual executives and their direct reports, then the performance metrics of the managers need to be reexamined.

itored—several modifications of the Identification and Justification Models have to be made to properly direct resources.

Just as a manager cannot acquire real-time information on every important metric simultaneously, so too it is highly unlikely that any organization can undertake real-time monitoring of all its most critical business processes simultaneously. Therefore, prioritization is essential. One of the key functions of the Identification and Justification Models is to prioritize information to be monitored in real time. Specifically, in the models, the manager goes through at least two prioritization filters, the first in step 2 of the Identification Model, where the manager prioritizes her various goals, the other in question 4 of the Justification Model, where the candidates for real-time monitoring are prioritized by their corporate impact. Corporate prioritizing, however, requires a slight modification to the models. In this case, rather than considering corporate impact as the last step, corporate impact is the mechanism for prioritizing goals in step 2 of the Identification Model. Perhaps the easiest way to perform this step is simply to examine the corporation's ten largest expense-generating or revenue-producing processes. Any process that does not have a direct impact on the corporate "top ten" should not be a focus of real-time opportunity detection across the enterprise. This is not to suggest that only information that affects the top ten revenue and expense items is worth monitoring in real time. However, information that does affect the "top ten" should be the highest priority by far and is the most appropriate place to begin spreading real-time opportunity detection. A side effect of this approach that should not receive short shrift is that due to the size and centrality of the "top ten," the path to transforming this information to real time also delivers real-time information on a large number of subprocesses, which allows many other managers to engage in predicting the present. This is yet another reason to focus prioritization on corporate impact.

The second modification to the Identification and Justification Models involves choosing the right metrics for measuring the prioritized corporate goals. The reason a change is necessary here is that the point of reference is no longer obvious. Recall that in chapter 2 we discussed the need to choose metrics that are accurate and can be consistently measured. We did not specifically discuss the need to choose meaningful and useful metrics because from the individual manager's perspective, they are self-evident (no manager would choose metrics he doesn't understand). However, when deploying real-time opportunity detection across the enterprise, there may be multiple executives or managers who could receive information about one of the core processes of the business, all of whom might choose a different metric to receive. Therefore, for each prioritized goal, a specific manager or executive needs to be chosen to be the point of reference; the proper metric to measure follows from that choice.

How should the point of reference be determined? Some inspiration for accomplishing this difficult task can be gained from an unlikely source, Roman Catholic social thought. One of the key principles of the Roman Catholic view of organizations is known as the principle of subsidiarity. It states that: "nothing should be done by a larger and more complex organization which can be done as well by a smaller and simpler organization."[1] Applying subsidiarity to the management process means that authority should be delegated to the lowest level capable of efficiently achieving the desired outcomes. The converse is true as well. Authority or responsibility should not be delegated below the managerial level best equipped to accomplish the goal. In this case, to determine the proper point of reference for real-time information on top corporate priorities, this question must be asked: Which recipient of the real-time information is capable of invoking the best possible response?

Let's return to our sushi boat from chapter 2 for an illustration. When last we visited, the captain had taken the first step in becoming a Real-Time Enterprise by monitoring refrigerant levels in real time. This allowed him to respond effectively to events that might have prevented his successfully meeting his most important goal—preserving the freshness of the fish in his hold. Let's imagine, however, that this sushi boat is just one of many in a fleet; the captain, rather than being the CEO of this enterprise, is just one of a number of senior managers working toward the overall corporate goal of delivering the most fresh tuna to the Tokyo markets. As this enterprise takes the second step to becoming a Real-Time Enterprise, the temptation will be to simply extend the existing real-time information to all other managers—in this case, to provide real-time refrigerant monitoring to every captain in the enterprise's fleet. Instead, when taking step 2, the point of reference of the real-time information should be reconsidered. Imagine that there is an admiral, the equivalent of a COO, who controls all the ships of this fishing enterprise. Imagine also that the admiral knows where all the ships in the fleet are. If the refrigeration system aboard any particular ship were to fail, the admiral could order the captain to rendezvous with another ship with a properly functioning refrigeration unit.

Here is where examining the point of reference really makes a difference. If the rendezvous could happen in four hours, then the metric being monitored must be reconsidered. In this case, monitoring temperature levels would provide ample time for an effective response (recall that spoilage takes twelve hours in our example). Therefore, step 2 for this fishing enterprise should not be equipping all its ships to monitor refrigerant levels. It should be shifting the focus of real-time efforts to provide real-time temperature monitoring across the fleet to the admiral. As an additional benefit, this practice may in fact be far less costly than providing real-time refrigerant level monitoring to many different captains.

At first glance, this may seem like a justification for limiting the flow of real-time information to only the most senior executives. In fact, it encourages the opposite. Deploying real-time temperature monitoring for the admiral also could provide this real-time information to every captain. (In fact, if the information is shared, the captains can now take on the "analyze" function (monitor, capture, analyze, report, respond), reporting real-time temperature information to the admiral only when it is outside the acceptable range.) Therefore, the proper application of the point-of-reference principle does not reinforce or condone limiting real-time information to a privileged few; rather, it encourages determining the most cost-efficient metrics and sharing the information widely. (Recall that in chapter 4 we saw the result of not reporting information widely in the Sears and Boeing examples—rather than eliminating surprises, surprises were magnified.)

Let's look at a more real-world example that also illustrates the need to choose the right metric for the chosen point of reference in the accounts payable process at a large public university (figure 6-1). An analyst in the finance department at the university, using the Identification and Justification Models, begins

FIGURE 6-1

A sample accounts payable process shows that executives and managers may need different metrics.

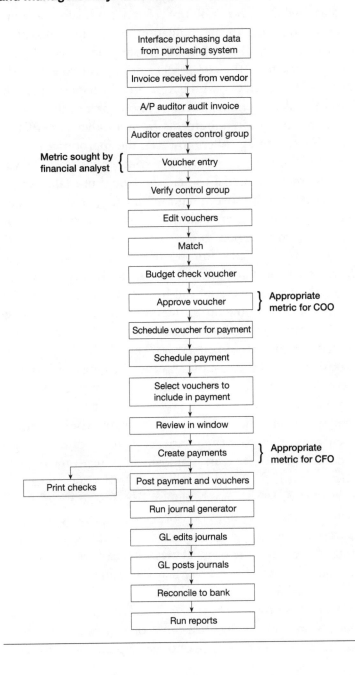

tracking voucher entries in real time, enabling him to meet budget-planning goals. However, once the university decides to take step 2 on the path to becoming a Real-Time Enterprise, it must evaluate who the best point of reference is for financial information of this sort. In the evaluation, it is determined that better responses to financial data not tracking on expected lines may be undertaken by the comptroller or provost (the equivalents of a CFO and COO), who have a broad perspective. Both positions can balance budget issues from one part of the organization against budget requirements from another part of the university. For the comptroller, however, the appropriate metric to monitor is not voucher entries but voucher approvals. Voucher entries are not material to her (she would not take action until a voucher was approved), and monitoring at the voucher approvals stage gives her enough time to schedule payments of those vouchers on a calendar appropriate to meet organizational goals. For the provost, the appropriate metric may be even farther downstream—create payments—as he finds only the actual disbursement of funds material and has enough time for appropriate responses. It is now up to these executives to determine who can best respond to the situation in a way that ensures the achievement of organizational goals. This decision may ultimately be dictated by the cost of capturing the data at any of the points considered (voucher entry, voucher approval, etc.).

As in these examples, when an organization begins spreading real-time opportunity detection across the enterprise, the point of reference and therefore the metrics monitored often change from what they were at the first deployment of real-time opportunity detection. This change should rarely lead to a repudiation of the original real-time monitoring effort. In the majority of cases, where there is a better point of reference, it simply means that aspects of the project need to be adjusted for maximum corporate benefit, and the original metrics measured may be replaced by another set of metrics either upstream or downstream in the process. Any new metric that is chosen for monitoring should, wherever possible, now be shared with the manager or managers who began the real-time opportunity detection process. In most cases they can continue to predict the present, even though their preferred metric may no longer be the focus. The more these enterprise metrics are shared, the greater the likelihood that all suspected events will be transformed to surmounted events.

Step 3: Overhaul Processes to Improve the Organization's Ability to Respond

The final step looks at the process of responding as a whole and focuses on removing all unnecessary and costly delays. While real-time opportunity detection will enable individual managers to have a positive impact on their organizations, for the organization as a whole to realize the maximum opportunities for success the real-time capture of critical data elements must join with revamped organizational structures, new management styles, and in many instances rebuilt business processes. The competitive advantage of Real-Time Enterprises will be the combination of the power of timelier monitoring and reporting of business events with the ability to respond to the events far more rapidly.

It can't be said often enough that even in the Real-Time Enterprise, responses are not necessarily made in real time (as noted in chapter 1, overly quick responses can be more harmful than helpful). The real change that happens in becoming a Real-Time Enterprise is that the ability to make a decision about the proper response and to implement that response is vastly improved.

Some have belittled the transformation to Real-Time Enterprise as just another version of business process reengineering. There is a kernel of truth here: The transformation requires the reengineering of many processes. Manual processes that impede the capture of real-time information (like those at Wet Seal and Amberwood Homes) have to be reengineered using technology. Beyond that, however, as part of improving its ability to respond, a Real-Time Enterprise does not just reengineer response processes for efficiency, it redesigns them to both take advantage of and generate real-time information that will allow even more real-time opportunity detection. This is not a minor point. Throughout the modern enterprise there are processes that function like black boxes—once a task is begun, it is impossible to tell what progress has been made until it is finished. All critical business processes need to be retrofitted to allow for near-continuous data collection about progress, if they are not already equipped to do so.

To clarify, let's return to the diagram used in chapter 1 to illustrate real-time opportunity detection (figure 6-2). Real-time opportunity detection focuses solely on ensuring that the right events are monitored and reported in real time to allow for the greatest number of response options, without examining the response process at all. Step 3 of the transformation to Real-Time Enterprise focuses on improving the response process: evaluating possible responses, deciding between possible responses, and implementing the response. As a result of the capability to respond faster, the number of response options grows again.

Earlier, we used the simple example of a sushi boat captain with a failed refrigeration unit to show how real-time detection increases possible responses. The example assumed that the captain could immediately come to a decision on the correct re-

FIGURE 6-2

Becoming a Real-Time Enterprise requires focus on an organization's ability to respond efficiently to events.

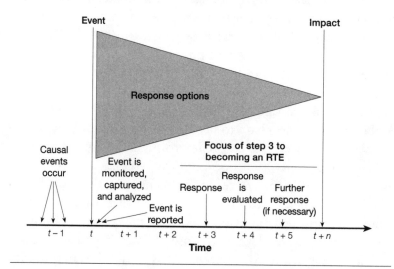

sponse and implement the chosen response without delay. In normal businesses, however, this process often takes weeks as meetings are scheduled and rescheduled, plans are devised and revised, and approval is sought. The example might be closer to business reality if the scenario developed as follows. The captain sees the failure of the refrigeration unit. He convenes a meeting of the crew to discuss the failure, its causes, and possible remedies. After several hours of discussion, consensus is reached to return to port. Further discussion is held to determine the best route back to port. Finally after the route is chosen, the response is launched.

Recall that in the original example, where the captain detects the failure of the refrigeration unit in real time, he does not have the option of returning to port because the trip would take more than twelve hours and his cargo of tuna would spoil before he reached his destination. Perhaps, however, the inability to reach port within the event–impact lag is not a factor of actual travel time but due to the fact that several hours are required to decide on and implement a response. If the response process were redesigned and these hours were saved, a response option that was impossible before would become available. Of course, the captain may not choose this response option, but it and other response options made possible by being able to respond faster raise the possibility that the response with the maximum benefit will be available and chosen. In the same way, managers who reengineer the response process broaden the response options available, further enhancing the success of the organization. This is the third step required to complete the transition to a Real-Time Enterprise.

A Word of Caution

Unfortunately, many managers will skip steps 1 and 2 entirely and focus only on step 3, reengineering response processes (while still using the name *Real-Time Enterprise*). This is not the same practice as undertaking steps 2 and 3 simultaneously. Many examples can be seen of companies that have focused their efforts on becoming more flexible and reacting faster to change. There are undeniable benefits to being able to react faster, but fast-reacting organizations can still be the victims of business surprises. Faster responses may in many cases allow an organization to escape a disaster due to an unanticipated market change, but occasions will arise where the change is not detected until after the impact is felt and faster responses are useful only for cleaning up after the fact. To use the driving analogy, focusing only on responding faster is akin to training yourself to step on the brakes faster and more forcefully rather than looking for ways to determine whether the traffic light has changed. Disaster is avoided by stopping in time, but the prevailing condition continues.

A manufacturer of consumer audio products (such as headphones) that is benefiting from improved response time without real-time opportunity detection provides an instructive example. The company, which we'll call Audio Inc. (not its real name), derived 97 percent of its revenues in fiscal year 2002 from the manufacture of consumer audio products. According to the CEO, approximately five years ago Audio Inc. was having difficulties manufacturing its products. On-time shipments of raw materials from abroad were infrequent, and the booming economy of the late 1990s made it difficult to find an adequate supply of labor to meet the demand for audio products. As a result of these supply and labor issues, Audio Inc.'s "just in time" manufacturing often ran behind demand. However, the issue that was the biggest surprise to the company was the tendency of its retail customers to order products in an inconsistent manner. "When I had large-scale intermediary orders where someone would decide to increase the number of items they wanted shipped to a distribution center, we couldn't respond to them," related the company's chief operating officer.[2] These and other external conditions resulted in a large volume of back orders at the end of nearly every month.

To reduce the delay in meeting customer orders and to avoid the cancellation of orders if prompt shipments did not occur, the executive team decided to dramatically improve the company's ability to respond by transforming the company's $15 million in inventory from raw materials to finished goods. Thus today, when Audio Inc. receives an order, the customer does not have to wait for the manufacture of the goods; the company responds with finished goods almost immediately, keeping valuable customers happy. Although sales improved (since the company did not have to turn down orders) and customer satisfaction rose, Audio Inc. was still vulnerable to surprises from, for example, a rapid slowdown in demand or rapidly falling parts prices. The company committed its resources so that it could be highly efficient at responding to one and only one event: a rise in orders. Thus, the company could not reap all the benefits possible for a Real-Time Enterprise.

Consider a similar contrast between the DEW Line and the Maginot Line. With the Maginot Line, France, prior to World War II, committed its forces not to detecting a possible invasion by Germany but to responding quickly to a specific invasion route (from the east). When the German invasion came from the north rather than the east, France was totally unable to mount a response. In contrast, the DEW Line focused on detection rather than response, which allowed the United States to defend against attacks other than a Soviet pole crossing. The military forces were able to use the same resources to respond to multiple possible threats.

The Struggle to Shift from Responding to Detecting

Perhaps the reason skipping to step 3 is so common is that most occupations and therefore business literature are focused on responses. Reducing all occupations to simple terms, almost all private sector occupational roles can be categorized in three business cycle phases: (1) before-sale activities, (2) sale activities, and (3) after-sale activities.

Before-sale activities take place before any product or service is sold. Examples include marketing to potential and existing customers and performing market research to ascertain customer behavior and demand. Sale-oriented activities include the efforts of the more than 13 million sales professionals who transform marketing, research, and other presale efforts into revenues. Finally, after-sale occupational efforts involve the fulfillment of products and services sold (service delivery, product creation, delivery of goods, and so on) as well as all the associated management, administrative, legal, training, and other activities that support fulfillment functions. A quick glance at the U.S. Labor Department's employment statistics (table 6-1) reveals that the vast majority of jobs fall into the third category.

If most people employed in the private sector are engaged in after-sale-oriented occupations, then it should be no surprise that most organizational and management attention, structures, theories, and practices pertain largely to the fulfillment effort after products and services have been sold. Because of this preponderance of after-sale activities, responding to events (for example, sales of products and services) has perhaps become second nature, if not encoded in our DNA. For managers to successfully guide their organizations in the transformation to Real-Time Enterprises, they must resist the temptation to stick with the change they are comfortable and familiar with and acquire a new mindset that recognizes the value of augmenting efforts to improve response-related endeavors with predicting the present and real-time opportunity detection.

Acquiring a new mindset and resisting the temptation to focus only on responding require a substantial commitment. Bringing about a successful outcome from such profound alterations to cultural norms could be among the most difficult tasks a person undertakes in his or her career. Because very few companies have begun the process of transforming to Real-Time Enterprises, very few executive teams know just how difficult the tasks are. However, the executive team at General Motors, led by CEO G. Richard (Rick) Wagoner, knows all about the difficulties involved in bringing cultural change to a company so that it can become a Real-Time Enterprise. If all goes well with the work Wagoner and his executives have accomplished so far, GM may become one of the best corporate examples of the benefits of taking all three steps required to become a true Real-Time Enterprise.

TABLE 6-1

2000 Employment by Occupational Title

Management	7,212,130
Business and financial operations	4,676,690
Office and administrative support	22,798,460
Computer and mathematical	2,825,820
Architecture and engineering	2,489,040
Life, physical, and social sciences	1,067,750
Community and social services	1,523,940
Legal	909,360
Education, training, and library	7,658,800
Arts, design, entertainment, sports, and media	1,508,730
Healthcare practitioners and technicians	6,118,880
Healthcare support	3,123,160
Protective service	2,958,050
Food preparation and serving	9,917,790
Building and grounds cleaning and maintenance	4,275,660
Personal care and service	2,801,640
Sales and related	13,418,770
Farming, fishing, and forestry	453,010
Construction and extraction	6,239,250
Installation, maintenance, and repair	5,322,980
Production	11,270,180
Transportation and material moving	9,410,340
Total	127,980,430

Source: Bureau of Labor Statistics, U.S. Department of Labor.

Early Warning

When Rick Wagoner was promoted from president of North American operations to chief operating officer in 1998, he knew that, despite the fact that GM was one of the ten largest corporations in the United States, its future was in doubt. His prior tenure in the finance department of GM, where he had worked his way up to the CFO position before taking on the North American role, had given him plenty of warning. The long and illustrious history of General Motors left it with a huge problem that few other companies, much less its chief foreign competition, shared—a huge number of retirees with guaranteed benefits. In fact, GM runs the largest private pension plan in the United States. In 1998 the plan was underfunded by $2 billion, meaning that the funds in the plan were not sufficient to meet expected future liabilities (figure 6-3).[3] To put that number in perspective, it is equivalent to the total annual revenues of retailer Bed, Bath and Beyond. The number is even more staggering when you consider that just five years earlier, the gap had been more than $18 billion and today exceeds $19 billion. (The changes from 1995 to 1998 and from 1998 to 2002 were primarily due to the bull and bear markets, respectively, although GM did contribute $40 billion in assets to the pension fund during the bull market.)

FIGURE 6-3

GM's pension fund deficit stood at nearly $20 billion in 2002.

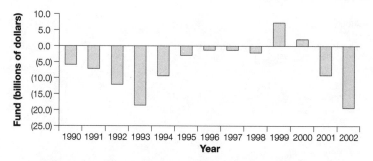

Source: General Motors, various SEC filings, all available at <http://www.gm.com/company/investor_information/sec/> (accessed 22 March 2003).

Additionally, GM's annual health care costs for its employees and retirees were more than $5 billion (more than the annual revenues of Owens Corning, Barnes & Noble, or Dole Food). According to Wagoner, "We have a huge fixed-cost base. It puts a premium on us running this business to generate cash."[4]

However, GM's prospects for running its business to generate cash did not look promising at the time. GM's U.S. market share had been on a steady decline for forty years, from 50 percent to less than 30 percent (figure 6.4).[5] Even worse, during the 1990s, GM's manufacturing productivity rating (measured by the number of person-hours required to build a car) fell well behind almost all other major manufacturers of cars and trucks, and the company trailed all other manufacturers in the major categories of manufacturing quality. On the whole, the picture was very dark: a desperate need for free cash flow, coupled with selling fewer vehicles at lower margins than the competition while eroding future growth possibilities by alienating buyers because of poor quality. None of this takes into account the

FIGURE 6-4

Beginning in 2001, GM's share of the domestic truck market increased for two consecutive years for the first time in more than a decade.

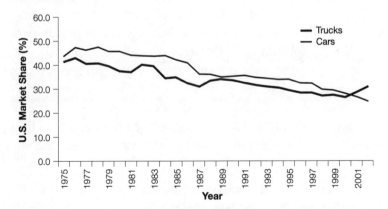

Source: American Automobile Manufacturers' Association, "Retail Market Share of Passenger Cars from General Motors Co.; Percent of U.S. Market (includes Saab starting in 1991)," available at <http://www.economagic.com/em-cgi/data.exe/aama/t4s3> (accessed 17 March 2003); General Motors, "Historical Market Share," Sales and Production presentation, <http://www.gm.com/company/investor_information/sales_prod/index.htm> (accessed 17 March 2003).

widespread criticism of GM's designs, which many consumers found boring or unappealing.

Although the time bomb of the pension plan underfunding would not explode for years, Wagoner recognized that even with the large event–impact lag, GM was not equipped to respond to the challenges it faced. A letter that crossed his desk shortly after his promotion to COO (Wagoner became CEO in 2000) clarified the path that GM had to take. "Someone sent my boss [Jack Smith, CEO of GM in 1998] a letter; he passed it on to me and I forwarded it to some people for a response. A month later, I finally get an answer back, and it's a draft letter back to the person who had originally written saying, 'Thank you for your suggestion. We want to study it for a month and get back to you.' It hit me like a ton of bricks. I thought, if all we were going to do is say we'll get back to you in a month, why couldn't we have sent that letter the next day? What happened here?"[6]

On the Road to the Real-Time Enterprise with GM

In short, the letter helped Wagoner realize that GM had to become a Real-Time Enterprise—and soon. The company did not have the luxury of slowly implementing change and watching improvement over time. GM had to see progress in real time to ensure that its cash needs were going to be met now and into the future. Thus, GM had to take all three steps to become a Real-Time Enterprise—(1) beginning real-time opportunity detection, (2) spreading RTOD throughout the enterprise, and (3) improving the organization's ability to respond—simultaneously, from real-time monitoring of quality to changing the corporate culture. Building on a decade's worth of efforts to improve productivity, GM began implementing the use of real-time information in two critical business processes: manufacturing and sales.

Steps 1 and 2 at GM: Boosting Productivity, Improving Quality, Regaining Sales

Two key groups of metrics help determine the overall effectiveness of the vehicle-manufacturing process: productivity and quality. The independent groups that the automotive industry

relies on most to measure quality and productivity are J. D. Power and Associates and Harbour and Associates, respectively. Both measurements must sustain alignment to make certain that one metric is not achieved at the expense of the other. According to Pat Morrissey, communications director for GM manufacturing: "If your quality is improving but your productivity is getting worse, all that means is you are putting more people in place to fix the problem."[7] That wouldn't help GM's cash needs. As Morrissey explained, the converse was equally unacceptable—continuing quality issues would obviate the need to produce more cars: No one would buy them.

GM faced a dilemma. The key industry metrics to measure productivity and quality provided by Harbour and J. D. Power are backward-looking. The J. D. Power results, for instance, are published annually, and therefore reveal the event of a quality defect well after the impact is felt—GM has another unhappy customer. GM executives realized that if they were to make gains in quality and productivity with the speed necessary, they needed real-time information on progress so that they could catch and respond to problems immediately. The efforts of the late 1990s had provided an infrastructure for real-time monitoring of productivity. To ensure that quality metrics had the same rigor and that any quality issues could be caught before they made it to customers, GM began tracking an internal quality measure, direct run rate, in real time in all its manufacturing plants. The primary intent of the direct run rate is to ensure that quality does not suffer in an attempt to improve productivity. To calculate the direct run rate, GM performs a quality inspection on each vehicle at three separate stages toward the end of the vehicle manufacturing and assembly process to determine the percentage of all vehicles that pass defect free through each of the three stages.[8] When all three results are determined, the individual results are multiplied to yield a final direct run rate:

Percent of defect-free vehicles at stage 1		Percent of defect-free vehicles at stage 2		Percent of defect-free vehicles at stage 3		Direct run rate
92%	×	90%	×	87%	=	72%

After enduring direct run rates in the 40 to 60 percent range in the mid-1990s (for example, vehicle quality results of 80% × 75% × 85% = 51 percent), in 2002 each of GM's twenty-eight manufacturing plants met or surpassed a direct run rate of 85 percent. As Gary Cowger, president of GM North America, described it: "You have to be running 95 percent plus good cars across the whole plant to be able to get an 85 percent direct run rate."[9] The key to this improvement was the wide distribution of real-time information about direct run rates.

To maintain constant awareness of the plant's direct run rate performance, large display panels were installed in every department of every assembly plant. As Morrissey explained, "The plant knows exactly what their direct run rate is at all times during the day. Any operator on the plant floor can see specifically what the plant is running for that day. And if there are problems, those are highlighted for their area as well." The system focuses attention on fixing problems immediately—the result was an immediate improvement in quality. In total, implementing this real-time quality- and productivity-tracking program enabled GM to build cars at a much faster rate with fewer employees at far better defect-free rates than at any other time in GM history—all critical to GM's ability to generate the cash it needs. To further its ability to monitor quality in real time and react to any flaws before the customer impact is felt, GM implemented the Andon system that originated in Japan (*andon* means "lantern" in Japanese) and is now used throughout the automotive industry. When a worker notices a defect in a part or assembly procedure as cars pass by on the assembly line, the worker has the option to pull an Andon cord to "illuminate" the problem. Pulling the cord immediately notifies the area supervisor that an issue warrants immediate attention and resolution. If the flaw is significant, the entire assembly line comes to a halt to prevent any additional flawed vehicles from advancing to the next assembly station.[10]

Another critical process that needed real-time monitoring was sales. As Wagoner stated in a 2003 *Business Week* interview, "[GM's] goal is to grow. We don't care who we take [market share] from."[11] Sales means something slightly different to GM executives than an outsider might imagine. GM's sales are to its network of dealers, not to car buyers. Wagoner implemented real-time tracking of dealer sales versus forecasts. This information is distributed widely in the sales group, but whereas Wagoner leaves direct run rate and productivity issues in the hands of Gary Cowger and other executives, he reviews the sales figures daily. He is now known to call relevant managers "immediately" when the reports reflect an unfavorable trend. "When sales results deviate from forecast for one day, I notice. If the forecast is still off the next day, I get a little concerned. If the forecast is off for a third day in a row, I'm on the phone asking, 'Hey, what's going on, guys, what are we doing?' I'm taking action based on sales reports at least once a week," says Wagoner.[12] Clearly, this metric is material to Wagoner. His attention has paid off: in 2001, GM gained North American market share for the first time in a decade; it improved again in 2002.

Step 3 at GM: Responding to Market Changes and Changing the Culture

As many organizations will do, GM simultaneously began working on redesigning its processes to deal with and provide real-time information as well as improving its ability to respond to real-time information. One critical business process that was totally unequipped to receive or provide real-time information, much less react effectively, was the process for designing new vehicles and putting them into production.

GM executives knew that the process for imagining, developing, building, and selling new car designs had needed a major overhaul since the early 1990s. The old process involved seven major steps:

1. Initial concept and design or redesign, a stage GM people refer to as the "gleam in the eye"

2. Detailed conceptual design, performed in GM's design studios

3. "Styling freeze," where the basic design of the car is approved and direction is given to produce the vehicle

4. Engineering, where detailed engineering and supplier specifications are determined, parts and assembly steps are specified, and factory retooling needs are finalized and implemented

5. Prototype and testing

6. Start of production, or manufacturing

7. Sales and distribution to dealer

When the first major effort to reduce the time involved in redesigning an existing model or creating an entirely new model began in 1996, it could take more than seventy-two months for a new design to become a purchasable product. As a result, GM's designs consistently lagged behind the market. Brands like Cadillac and Buick that had once set the style and design tone for the entire industry now released cars that looked five years old the day they were introduced. The design process itself was labyrinthine; even insiders couldn't keep track of where any particular design was in the process. In the mid-1980s GM had decentralized its design process by creating a number of separate, autonomous divisions that would oversee their own respective vehicle design and manufacturing efforts.[13] It was not long after the decentralization that executives realized that whatever problems they hoped to resolve by decentralization were replaced with new issues. As Gary Cowger put it: "We ended up with all kinds of people developing cars and designing manufacturing systems across the company and that was creating huge problems."

Once a vehicle design had been finished and approved, it had to pass through a gauntlet of competing groups responsible for turning the design into a vehicle that could be mass produced. This process involved more than twenty different incompatible computer-aided design (CAD) software packages being used by more than ten different groups, none of whom had total authority to make a decision when a conflict came up. The vehicles

that made it past this stage still had to pass through the manufacturing process, which began with determining how to set up
a factory to make the particular car.

To cut the time required for GM to respond to market
changes with new vehicles, executives would have to significantly streamline each of the major steps. Aggressive goals were set
to cut both the first and second phases of development in half
by 2002. According to Wagoner, the effort to shorten the inter-
val between "gleam in the eye" and styling freeze, illustrated in
figure 6-5, really made progress when Robert Lutz joined GM
as the new head of product development. Lutz "took a lot of
people out of the process, engaged the design people sooner,
and connected the various functions earlier in the process."[14] A
major breakthrough was made when Lutz appointed a single executive to oversee the entire process, which cut a huge amount
of time from the design process by accelerating the decision
making during the conceptual and early design phase.

Reducing the time of the next major phase of development,
from styling freeze to start of production, took several steps,
first among them standardizing the IT environment to streamline collaboration. GM upgraded and standardized communica-

FIGURE 6-5

**GM reduced the time for the design and manufacturing
process considerably between 1995 and 2000.**

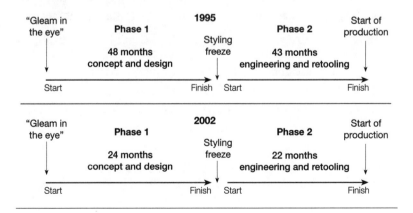

tions and computer systems around the world. The twenty-plus different CAD systems were replaced with a single design environment that became GM's global standard. (This global IT effort was facilitated after GM hired its very first chief information officer, Ralph Szygenda, in 1996).

Executives also realized that they would have to make organizational changes in this part of the process if they were to reach their goals. Therefore, GM began recentralizing engineering activities to create a more consistent way of designing and especially manufacturing cars across the company. According to Jerry Elson, vice president of vehicle operations in North America, "In 1992 there were seven groups making vehicles. By 2000 there were two, cars and trucks. In 2001, those two groups were combined into one."[15] Finally, GM reduced decision-related delays by putting a vehicle line executive in charge of each product. These executives were granted the authority to make vital decisions, thus eliminating some of the bureaucracy for which GM had become so famous.

All these efforts began to pay off dramatically in 2001. According to James Queen, GM vice president of North America engineering, by midwinter 2003 GM's gap had reached 22.8 months, with some styling freeze to start of production programs scheduled for 18 months and two scheduled for 12 months.[16] Mr. Queen was particularly proud that "one of [those programs] is a completely brand new car, from the ground up." Queen stated, "In the 12-month program . . . we're bypassing the whole prototype stage. We're going directly to production tools." Queen's group is not only moving faster, it has become remarkably more efficient. He estimated that in 2002 his group completed 30 percent more projects than in the past, despite cutting their budget by 46 percent compared to 1997.

Gary Cowger sees the efforts bearing fruit across the whole design and build process. "The metrics on changing over a plant used to be that you would be down for a major [overhaul for a totally new or a completely redesigned vehicle] for three or four months, and today, we can do a major [plant overhaul] on our flexible body shops over a couple of weeks and have the ability to build the old product while slowly ramping up the new product."

By redesigning the vehicle design process, GM is now able to respond much faster to changes in the market environment, the core of step 3. Just as important, the streamlined process is beginning to generate real-time information on progress, enabling the beginnings of real-time opportunity detection in this critical business process.

Redesigning the manufacturing and design processes to use and produce real-time information was not enough, Wagoner knew.[17] The culture of the entire organization, embodied in his anecdote about the letter, had to change if GM was to consistently respond effectively to the events now being detected. Wagoner was specifically concerned that people would adopt changes that he mandated and not internalize the need for the change—and that therefore any changes would last only as long as his direct attention was focused on a particular project. Instead, he wanted people to move faster from their own recognition that greater speed was essential to the future of the company. Wagoner was looking for a massive shift of the corporate culture that had moved too slowly for far too long and was burdened with years of blindly following legacy processes within a lethargic and crippling bureaucracy. To accomplish this goal, Wagoner launched the GoFast! program.

GM's GoFast! program officially began in 1999 and borrowed heavily from General Electric's Work-Out program, launched in 1988. GE describes the Work-Out program as follows:

Initially, Work-Out was intended to identify and eliminate unneeded processes and tasks that were left over from previous years, when management had more layers. After restructuring, many groups did more work with fewer people, rather than making comprehensive operational changes.

The aptly named Work-Out process involves identifying an area in need of improvement and bringing people together from all sides of the process (design, marketing, production, sales, etc.) to identify a better method. The Work-Out team meets outside of its normal work environment to discuss the issues and develop recommendations.

Team recommendations are presented to the responsible managers, who must accept or reject proposals on the spot. Ideas that require further study are reviewed for a period of time agreed on by the team (usually less than a month) before a final decision is made. The process encourages responsive leadership and greater employee participation, which increases the rate of change throughout the organization.[18]

GM followed GE's Work-Out formula nearly to the letter. Each workshop is intensely focused on the work performed by a specific group and the remedies that will be carried out by that specific group. Wagoner's obsession with bringing speed to GM is reflected in the one major point where GM's GoFast! program differs from GE's Work-Out. GM chose to hold one-day workshops rather than the three-day meetings GE favored. Additionally the relative brevity of each meeting forced the departments to prioritize the issues that most needed to be addressed and resolved.

Not surprisingly, those who had spent many years within the culture at GM gave the GoFast! program mixed reviews, but Wagoner kept up the pressure. "Last year I told all of our top four hundred leaders to personally sponsor at least two GoFast sessions and e-mail me the recommendations of the session. I read and responded to all e-mails I received."[19] In the initial phase, however, results were mixed. In the first year, only three hundred of the expected eight hundred sessions had been conducted. Wagoner relentlessly pursued those who had not yet conformed to the edict in a continuing effort to convey a sense of urgency to reduce delay and bureaucracy within the company. He even created the GoFast! Hub to assist in setting up and running workshops. Since that time GM has conducted more than 8,000 GoFast! workshops.

The GoFast! program comes into play in the manufacturing arena when workers from the manufacturing departments meet to consider the quality concerns revealed in the annual J. D.

Powers and Associates initial quality study. The workshops are used to fully understand the issues identified in the study and to quickly determine how to resolve the problems uncovered. Years ago, quality issues would be resolved only after weeks or months of meetings and other bureaucratic steps. Today, when workers and managers leave a one-day GoFast! meeting, they know the steps that will be taken to resolve the issue.

The actions that are taken as a result of each and every Go-Fast! workshop are not expected to individually contribute vast amounts of cost savings or yield dramatic improvements in productivity and quality. Instead, the output of the workshops is intended to bring an end to the bureaucratic and unresponsive cultural traits that have plagued GM for decades. By changing this culture, GM is building the foundation for improving all its decision making and reactions to events, top to bottom. Combining real-time opportunity detection with an improved ability to respond to events as they are detected is bringing the cost savings, faster product development, higher margins (due to higher productivity and quality), and increased sales that the company so desperately requires.

Power of the Real-Time Enterprise

General Motors is one of the first companies to begin experiencing the power of bringing together the use of real-time opportunity detection across the entire enterprise *and* enabling much faster responses. The results, even at this early stage, are dramatic. On top of growing market share, General Motors has increased quality and productivity simultaneously, cut costs, and introduced an average of one new vehicle per month in 2003.

The best evidence of GM's success so far is in the 2002 Harbour and Associates report on automobile manufacturing. Each year, Harbour and Associates Inc., an independent consultancy located in Troy, Michigan, issues a report highlighting the annual manufacturing performance of the major automotive manufacturers in North America, including DaimlerChrysler, Honda, Toyota, Ford, and of course, GM.

Following are excerpts from the 2002 Harbour Report (and a summary appears in table 6-2). A J. D. Power report backs up Harbour's data (table 6-3).

GM, with a 4.5% overall improvement, led the domestic manufacturers in assembly, engine and transmission productivity, which marked the first time in the history of The Harbour Report that GM finished ahead of Ford in the assembly and overall hours per vehicle (HPV) measures. Also for the first time ever, a GM plant (Oshawa #1, with a 16.79 HPV) led all North American car and truck plants in assembly productivity.

. . .

At long last, the company's systems and processes are paying off in improved productivity, higher quality—as shown recently in the company's improved performance in J. D. Power's initial quality scores—and lower costs.

. . .

TABLE 6-2

GM Productivity Improvements

Class	Vehicles	2001 HPV	1997 HPV
Midsize car plant	Chevrolet Impala and Monte Carlo	16.79	20.18
Compact car plant	Pontiac Grand Am and Oldsmobile Alero	20.11	24.06
Best full-size SUV Plant	Chevrolet Tahoe and Suburban, GMC Yukon and Yukon XL, and Cadillac Escalade	25.99	40.75
Best luxury car plant	Buick LeSabre and Cadillac DeVille and Seville	29.47	48.99
Best full-size truck plant	Chevrolet Silverado and GMC Sierra	20.95	24.09
Best minivan plant	Chevrolet Venture, Pontiac Montana, and Oldsmobile Silhouette	25.00	31.96

Source: Harbour and Associates Inc., *Harbour and Associates 2001 Report.*

TABLE 6-3

GM Efficiency Scores in Relation to Other Manufacturers (Assembly Workers per Vehicle)

Manufacturer	1992	2001
Daimler Chrysler	3.76	3.54
Ford	3.10	3.27
Honda	2.53	2.40
General Motors	4.55	2.96
Nissan	2.20	2.18
Toyota	2.64	2.40

Source: Rick Wagoner, "Taking GM to the Next Level, Leveraging Strengths, Addressing Challenges, Focusing on the Future" (presentation to securities analysts, teleconference, 9 January 2003). Data are from J.D. Power and Associates, <www.jdpower.com> (accessed 15 February 2003).

General Motors produced some notable achievements in assembly manufacturing. Three GM car plants . . . led their respective segments, as did three of the company's truck plants . . . And seven of the 10 most improved plants were GM operations, led by Flint Assembly, which was the most improved plant in the report. After moving ahead of Ford and Auto Alliance, GM finished sixth overall in the company productivity rankings. In the last two years alone, GM has improved its HPV by nearly 4 hours.[20]

Rick Wagoner and his team are not done yet. Each of the executives perceive more opportunities for monitoring critical information in real time and further improving response times. Wagoner cites a desire for more frequent information on projects in the early part of design. "I think if we had a little more live status of product programs, it would probably help."[21] Jerry Elson believes that he can cut the time required for the second phase of vehicle production by another 30 percent, allowing even better responses to market shifts.

Conclusion

The progress of General Motors is remarkable, and it hints at the power Real-Time Enterprises will have to rapidly improve their market position and exert tremendous pressure on their competitors. While DaimlerChrysler and Ford struggled, GM grew sales 5 percent, doubled its operating profit year over year, and regained the top market share position in the truck market, which produces the highest margins in the industry. Still, the success of General Motors is not assured. The cash requirements of the pension fund and healthcare expenses will keep growing—GM has more retirees and beneficiaries than it does active workers. The number of retirees (including spouses) who are eligible to receive GM pension and post-retirement benefits will continue to increase until at least 2008. We know that the cash need of General Motors is *definitely not* a surprise event. The company successfully advanced beyond the surprise event stage in the 1990s after executives saw the warning signs of pension underfunding and the quality, productivity, and market share loss problems that had grown in severity throughout the 1970s and 1980s. Although it is clear how real-time methodologies helped (for instance) eBay avoid a number of major public relations disasters and Amberwood increase its margins, whether real-time methodologies will help GM's pension funding become a surmounted event instead of a suspected event is still uncertain and will be for years to come. However, because of GM's ongoing efforts as a Real-Time Enterprise work in progress, taking all three steps by combining real-time opportunity detection with new organizational structures, a modified culture, and an ability to respond much more quickly, current indications suggest that General Motors could become one of the greatest success stories of the emerging era of Real-Time Enterprises.

7

solving the challenges of deploying real-time opportunity detection

ONE OF THE MOST CONTENTIOUS TOPICS in business organization and development today is globalization. Horst Kohler, managing director of the International Monetary Fund, describes globalization as "a process of increasing international division of labor and the accompanying integration of national economies through trade in goods and services, cross-border corporate investments, and financial flows."[1]

Economists and corporate leaders defend the benefits of globalization and a wide variety of groups protest against its drawbacks, but there can be no question that the economies of all but the least developed nations are globalized, responding rapidly to economic events around the world via flows of labor and capital. The impact of globalization had never been felt more intensely than in 1997 and 1998, when the sudden and surprise collapse of Asian financial markets was instantly seen not only in the region but around the world. A survey of American Fortune 500 companies would undoubtedly show that nearly 100 percent of them claimed a negative impact on revenues or earnings due to the economic turmoil in Asia. Remarkably, according to Stanley Fischer, first deputy managing director of the International Monetary Fund at the time, the process of events that would hobble giant corporations and slow the largest national economies began in Thailand:

> Starting in 1996, a confluence of domestic and external shocks revealed weaknesses in the Thai economy that until then had been masked by the rapid pace of economic growth and the weakness of the U.S. dollar to which the Thai currency, the baht, was pegged. . . .
>
> Past success may also have contributed to a sense of denial among the Thai authorities about the severity of Thailand's problems and the need for policy action, which neither the IMF in its continuous dialogue with the Thais during the 18 months prior to the floating of the baht last July, nor increasing exchange market pressure, could overcome. Finally, in the absence of convincing policy action, and after a desperate defense of the currency by the central bank, the crisis broke.[2]

Once the Thai economy came under pressure from the rapid devaluation of the Thai bhat, concern soon spread about Thailand's neighbors, including Indonesia, Malaysia, Singapore, and South Korea. The resulting crisis of confidence in Asian economies spread around the world as companies based in these countries lost access to capital, which caused them to stop buying imported goods, and companies headquartered in the West cut back on investments and jobs. Many companies were taken utterly off guard by the crisis, if for no other reason than that they had no idea that their economic outlook depended on the actions of the Thai central bank.

One of the core premises of this book is that there is no such thing as a business surprise. Indeed, as Stanley Fischer indicates in his comments, there was warning of what would happen in Thailand and anyone with an average level of familiarity with international capital and currency markets could have foreseen the likely outcome of a dramatic devaluation of the Thai currency. However, it is disingenuous to suggest that in today's globalized world, all the companies that might be impacted by financial problems in Asia are currently capable of keeping track of monetary and fiscal policy in Thailand and its neighbors. For the vast majority of managers in corporate America, the chains of antecedent events that the Identification Model advocates following would disappear into hazy uncertainty before they arrived at the metrics that might have alerted them to the coming crisis. Once the crisis broke, it spread so quickly that even real-time monitoring of Japanese financial markets may not have provided an event–impact lag long enough for an appropriate response.

New Roles, New Responsibilities

As companies begin to take the second and third steps toward becoming a Real-Time Enterprise, deploying real-time opportunity detection in all their most critical business processes and improving their ability to respond to the events thereby detected, they will run into issues like the Asian financial crisis more and more often. Even with a majority of managers engaging in real-time opportunity detection, some events, like the Asian financial crisis, that are critical to the organization's success may not be monitored. Similar to the situation at Boeing documented in chapter 5, although some managers may be monitoring events in real time, crucial information may not be passed to all relevant parties. In other organizations, the intersection of processes governed by real-time opportunity detection with those that are not yet real time will cause confusion and inefficiency. Changing a company's critical business processes to operate in real time, to provide up-to-date feedback on progress when necessary to truly end all business surprises, requires that the most senior executives of a corporation take an active role in the transformation. Specifically, it requires that they take on three new roles to successfully navigate steps 2 and 3 of the path to becoming a Real-Time Enterprise: (1) Real-Time Enterprise change leader, (2) long-distance lookout, and (3) internal monitor and reporter.

Real-Time Enterprise Change Leader

Transforming into a Real-Time Enterprise is not an overnight process, and many challenges will have to be overcome. Perhaps the first of these functions to be appropriated, as senior executives realize the enterprisewide scope of these challenges, will be Real-Time Enterprise change leader. In many cases, the function will begin to evolve as an extension of the duties of an existing senior executive, most commonly chief operating officer, chief information officer, or chief financial officer. As executives develop strategies to enable real-time opportunity detection across the enterprise, they will encounter two related categories of obstacles: (a) IT challenges and (b) process challenges.

IT Challenges

The information technology challenges to developing real-time enterprises are relatively straightforward and easy to see, if not easy to overcome. The information needed to predict the present and enable real-time opportunity detection is collected and stored in IT systems. At many companies, these systems still rely on far less than real-time updates of the necessary information. One of the changes required is enabling the capture of an event as it happens. Doing so will often mean replacing a time-consuming manual process with technology. For instance, many companies will begin by assessing how to capture a sale or an order change the moment it happens. In the vast majority of cases outside the rapidly changing retail industry, there is a significant gap between actual sale and the capture of the information because of lengthy, often manual, recording processes. For example, the sales booking process of many professional services firms involves a field salesperson getting a contract signed at the client site, carrying the contract back to an office, and faxing the contract to a central order entry location where another person collects the faxed information and manually inputs the contract information into another system.

In the worst-case scenario, several additional delays are possible, such as the contract not being complete, not all pages being received, data being entered incorrectly, and so on. In all too many instances, it can be weeks before the correct information is properly entered, not to mention further time before those responsible for planning service delivery are notified. An increasingly common solution to this problem will be the one Amberwood Homes used: wireless technology. A foreman enters construction status on a wireless personal digital assistant (such as a Palm Pilot) and the information is immediately updated in the company's central database; the foreman is not required to fill out forms and carry them by hand or phone them back to the office for reentry. Wireless information collection technologies like those Amberwood uses, as well as the rapidly growing use of radio frequency identification (RFID) tags for material goods (which allow even small items to be tracked without manual intervention), will be the primary tools for solving the data collection challenge.

Although solving the data collection challenge is an important first step, it is not the only technology challenge organizations will have to meet. Organizations will also have to deal with the delays found in systems that continue to rely on batch processing. Rather than executing each transaction as it happens, these systems store all transactions for a certain amount of time and then process them together at the end of the day, the end of the week, or even the end of the month. Accounts payable and receivable, perhaps more than any other function, still heavily rely on batch processing. Modern enterprise resource-planning systems implemented by many organizations as they upgraded in anticipation of year 2000 vastly decreased the number of systems reliant on batch processing but did not eliminate them. Batch-processing systems are also prevalent where two systems have to interact, for instance where manufacturing systems pass inventory information to customer relationship management systems. Internet technologies, including XML, Web services, application integration tools, and disciplines, will have the greatest impact in eliminating batch processing and enabling real-time monitoring.

Finally, organizations will have to deal with data integration—agreeing on common metrics and measurements to bring together data from across the corporation so that it can be evaluated as a whole. Data integration is only indirectly a technology issue in that it will require changes to database management and business intelligence systems that are already in place. The larger part of this challenge will be gaining agreement across the enterprise to use and conform to standard metrics and measures. Enterprises that have already started down the path of corporate performance management with tools like the Balanced Scorecard will have an advantage in overcoming this challenge because they will in large part already have dealt with consolidating on core metrics. However many organizations that have reached the level of intellectual assent are still converting data manually so that they can be plugged into Balanced Scorecards and other operations management tools. Until this challenge is overcome, true Real-Time Enterprises cannot exist.

Process Challenges

GM's vice president of North American vehicle operations, Jerry Elson, noted that 90 percent of GM's gains to date in speeding up vehicle design have been process rather than technology related.[3] Similarly, technology will often only be a small part of the overall challenge faced by the transforming organization. The bigger challenge will be revamping inefficient processes. With the right technology in place, the number of processes that are inherently inefficient will suddenly become much clearer, but attempts to fix these processes may often result in poor or expensive outcomes rather than the benefits expected. Americans' twenty-year love affair with home alarm systems provides an instructive example. During the 1980s, as the technology that enables home alarms and central monitoring became more affordable, the number of installed systems rose dramatically. Alarm companies very effectively marketed the "fast response" benefit—when an alarm was triggered the central monitoring station would call police and/or the fire department and help would be on its way. Undeniably, lives have been saved and tragedies have been prevented by these systems; insurance companies recognized this and began offering discounted rates on home owner's insurance if an alarm system was present. Recently, however, there has been a backlash against these alarms led by municipalities. The highest-profile action taken to date has been the January 2003 decision by the city of Los Angeles that officers will not respond to any alarm that has not been visually verified—by video cameras installed in the home or by the direct observation of an alarm company employee or neighbor. The policy was developed after a Justice Department study in 2002 found that false alarms cost local police departments $1.5 billion and the time of 35,000 officers. Additionally, the LAPD felt that false alarms were preventing them from effectively responding to and protecting homes without alarm systems. The new approach is an extension of earlier efforts that made responding to alarms the lowest priority for police units.[4]

The lesson here is that adjusting processes to fit real-time information may yield immediate improvements that mask damage to other parts of an organization. This situation will occur with surprising frequency in the early stages of Real-Time Enterprise development, especially whenever ease of implementation overcomes corporate impact when determining priorities. Many organizations and executives will not have the discipline to focus their real-time efforts on transforming items dictated by corporate impact (see the discussion of modifying the Identification Model for corporate use in chapter 6) and will settle instead for transforming only metrics and processes that require little additional effort. The net result will be similar to the experience of police departments with home alarm systems—by improving one process they will harm another. The largest organizational challenge will be determining which processes need to be changed in what order for results to be achieved. Taking a systemwide view is crucial for effectively managing process improvements. Therefore, it is critical that an executive, who can

PEOPLE CHALLENGES

Companies that are developing real-time opportunity detection and beginning the transition to being Real-Time Enterprises will also face another significant structural challenge. As in every major organizational change, there will be challenges in changing ingrained behaviors and work styles. Ron Hunt, operations manager at Wet Seal, commented, "When we first began delivering the real-time sales reports to the district and region managers, we quickly realized that many of them weren't sure what to do with the information. We had to organize training sessions to help them understand the reports and to guide them in what conclusions were or were not valid based on the data that were being delivered."[5]

The greatest change will be required of organizations and managers who adhere to strict hierarchical command and control structures. In environments where decision-making authority is closely held, there are only two possible outcomes: managers will have to delegate authority to a level they have typically not been comfortable with, or they must become "always on," able to be contacted for decisions at any time of day on any day of the year whenever real-time information demands a decision. Indeed, no matter what the decision-making environment, the prevalence of real-time information will further blur the work–life separation and create intense people management challenges.

Additionally, managers will struggle to learn new ways of dealing with information. Some will compensate for the newfound insight delivered by real-time information by overreacting; others will delay needed decisions, hoping that the next minute will reveal information that obviates the need for action. The transition will not be easy and every employee will need to adjust to new organizational constructs and new work styles. Compensation plans will have to be reviewed and adjusted to ensure that compensation is not tied to "old," non-real-time processes.[6] Where people failures limit the success of Real-Time Enterprise efforts, this challenge will often necessitate the appointment of an individual or an office, similar to the General Motors GoFast! office, to train, coach, and lead personnel in the required cultural changes.

look over the entire corporate system, take on this function. Anything less will lead to suboptimal and perhaps even damaging results as resources are not focused or directed appropriately.

On the positive side, incredible benefits will accrue to those executives who stick to their guns, focus their energies on the right priorities, and battle through the effort to transform the business processes that stand in the way of predicting the present. Such process improvements will deliver several benefits in addition to the benefits of detecting potential problems or opportunities in advance (see, for example, the side benefits achieved by Amberwood Homes and Wet Seal in chapter 5). First, the drive for real-time opportunity detection will usher in a new phase of productivity gains in business processes, many of which have been so far insufficiently enhanced or perhaps even untouched by technology. Second, productivity gains will help keep employee output at levels ahead of wage increases, keeping the employee cost index in check, which will enhance profitability and competitive positioning.

Long-Distance Lookout

On February 27, 2003, Federal Reserve chairman Alan Greenspan testified before the Senate Special Committee on Aging about the looming dangers of demographic change for the American economy. Mr. Greenspan told senators that as the American population ages and the baby boomer generation begins to retire around 2013, the current Social Security system will be overwhelmed—there will be too few workers to support the much larger number of retirees. He strongly urged the Congress to take action now to alter benefits when the transition can be smooth rather than when the system reaches a crisis and changes would be "abrupt and painful."[7] The next day, the front page of the *Wall Street Journal*'s Marketplace section ran three stories about global demographic change that will drastically impact business planning over the next half-century at least. Two of the stories were about the demographics of age in developed versus developing nations, while a smaller item noted the United Nations' revision of its forecast of the population impact of AIDS.[8] It does not take much consideration to realize that the global economic environment will be changed by these population trends. However, it will take significant and constant attention and planning to determine exactly what those changes might be and how they will affect individual companies.

Greenspan's comments highlighted an issue that governments and business share: Few, if any, governments or businesses have the capability to truly examine changes that may be up to a decade in the future and respond to the expected changes. The changes are too far in the future for the sustained attention required for developing effective response strategies when there are so many other issues that demand attention in the near term. As a result, far too many businesses and governments will not begin to plan responses now while the event–impact lag is still large and many, many response options are possible. These organizations will not react until it is too late for anything but "abrupt and painful" responses.

It is exactly this inability that requires the creation of a function specifically for looking beyond and behind immediate corporate concerns. Now more than ever, companies must create the ability to look far beyond the boundaries of corporate headquarters for events that create opportunity or portend problems. The function of long-distance lookout will call for focus on following event–impact chains much further back than the average manager can or has the time to do.

One of the mantras hammered into the brains of young political science students is "Correlation does not imply causation." In other words, simply because two things happen in succession does not mean that the first caused the second. This kind of flawed reasoning has been seen on many occasions in the recent history of genomics. Scientists have falsely concluded that certain genes "cause" certain diseases and then discovered after testing that the reality is far more complex (it is not a single gene but twenty different genes interacting that actually "cause" the disease). As enterprises attempt to deploy real-time opportunity detection to all critical business processes, it will be common for executives and managers to make the mistake of monitoring events that they believe will have a specific impact because of correlation rather than causation. Ron Hunt at Wet Seal noticed this phenomenon in the early stages of Wet Seal's deployment of real-time reports, "Managers were so interested in monitoring real-time sales trends that at the beginning they would often forget to correlate the sales data with the purchasing data—they would conclude that a certain item wasn't popular because relatively few had been sold without comparing that to the number of items that had originally been distributed. It was a simple mistake."[9] Simply by virtue of being mandated to test hypotheses, people who take on the function of long-distance lookout will be able to determine what the true cause–impact chain looks like and better prepare the organization to monitor the metrics that will enable correct predictions of the present. Indeed, this advantage of the long-distance lookout will not only reveal situations where the cause–impact chains are more complicated than they seem originally; it will also lead to the discovery of cause–impact chains that have been entirely overlooked. Thus, the long-distance lookout must specialize in drawing connections between seemingly unrelated information—her focus on monitoring all relevant information will allow her to see both correlations and causal events overlooked in the past.

Finally, the long-distance lookout will also need to advise on when earlier detection of precursor events is impossible or too costly because of current technology limitations. The organization can then focus attention on accelerating reporting, decision-making, and response capability so that when the earliest possible event is detected, the organization can maximize the event–impact lag for successful results.

The news industry provides a perfect example. If you walk into any major television news organization today, somewhere in the office you will discover obituary videos, tributes to the famous and infamous, reviewing their careers and achievements. You may be startled to find, however, that the obituaries are for people who are still living. Years ago, news organizations realized that they could not detect the death of celebrities any sooner, yet if they could not nearly instantaneously provide a retrospective, the organization would lose an immensely valuable opportunity to connect with viewers. Thus, the decision was made to ensure that an effective response could be mounted in the limited event–impact lag possible—and the obituaries of the living were created, ready to be broadcast within minutes of detecting the death of famous entertainers, politicians, and icons. It will be incumbent on the long-distance lookout to determine when to focus attention on capturing the earliest possible event in a cause–impact chain and when to shift attention to responding faster, thus effectively balancing the steps necessary to become a Real-Time Enterprise. Again, it is clear that the long-distance lookout function, just like the Real-Time Enterprise change leader function, must be taken on by an executive.

There are several business trends that will drive organizational realization of the need for a long-distance lookout. Globalization, referred to earlier, means that more companies depend more on economic conditions in more countries around the world. As figure 7-1 shows, many U.S. companies derive more than 40 percent of their revenues from outside the United States. As the dependence on suppliers and customers increases beyond a company's native borders, risk levels to company performance and health also rise dramatically. Unfavorable changes to nondomestic customer demand, currency exchange rates, laws, business, accounting and financial disclosure practices, and so on can easily contribute to a sudden revenue shortfall, increase in costs, missed earnings, or unforeseen litigation, as well as a host of other harmful impacts.

As the Asian financial crisis proved, companies that hope for long-term success must have an eye on the international climate and how it might affect not only their business but the business of their chief suppliers and customers. The most savvy long-distance lookouts will also begin monitoring the status of their closest competitors' clients and their clients' clients as well (not to mention suppliers), looking for real-time opportunities to capitalize on weaknesses. Note that the DEW Line was an early example of extending monitoring to "partners"—most of the line runs across Canada.

FIGURE 7-1

Many large U.S. corporations earn more than 40 percent of their revenue in other countries, making monitoring of political and economic policy abroad vital to success.

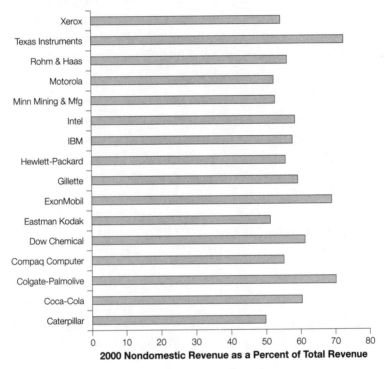

Source: Megan E. Mulligan, "The International 500," *Forbes,* 23 July 2001, 38.

A second major trend that creates the need for a person who is looking far down cause–impact chains is outsourcing. In 1990, C. K. Prahalad and Gary Hamel published one of the most influential business articles written in the 1990s. In that article they stated:

During the 1980s top executives were judged on their ability to restructure, declutter and delayer their corporations. In the 1990s, they'll be judged on their ability to identify, cultivate and exploit the core competencies that will make growth possible—indeed, they'll have to rethink the concept of the corporation itself.[10]

Thousands of executives used Prahalad and Hamel's *Harvard Business Review* article as a guide in transferring a number of noncritical business functions from their companies to firms that specialized in such activities. While alternative sourcing has existed for many years, the list of business functions company executives have outsourced since 1990 has been considerable. Here is just a partial list:

Accounting services	Life, health, and medical
Auditing services	insurance
Advertising services	Travel and reservation
Call center services	services
Credit card	Marketing
intermediation	Media buying
Event management	Office and administrative
services	services
Human resources	Executive search services
Information technology	Public relations
services	Rental and leasing services
Legal services	Research and survey services
Teaching and training	Telemarketing

Most companies devise alternative sourcing strategies as a way to (1) encourage growth through saving money, (2) encourage agility and maintain the focus of management attention on the core issues facing the company, (3) avoid having to hire people with expertise not easily found, and (4) improve service levels to customers. But what happens when one of these alternative sourcing companies fails to deliver services or goods that are of the highest quality or conducts business dealings that are not of the highest ethical standards?

When Company A transfers operational fulfillment of a business function over to Company B, Company A loses control over how the function is performed unless strict vigilance is maintained. Best practices in sourcing contracts dictate specifying oversight; companies then must undertake the required vigilance to make sure goals and metrics are met. Few companies follow best practices, however, and fewer maintain watches on the other customers and business practices of their outsourcers that are not directly linked to them, much less other factors that might affect business continuity for processes that are outsourced. Never was this gap better illustrated than in the fall of 2002 when the collapse of Arthur Andersen followed on the heels of a dramatic rise in tensions between Pakistan and India in late 2001 and early 2002. The countries were at the brink of what very likely might have been nuclear war, and panic enveloped many large companies that had outsourced significant operations to India but had failed to monitor the political situation. Suddenly thousands of organizations were trying to develop contingency plans for a war that might have come at any time. Shortly thereafter, many of the same companies had to scramble to replace consultants and auditors from Arthur Andersen when the firm collapsed after allegations of wrongdoing at a few companies that Andersen audited. When a corporation begins outsourcing major business processes, it can benefit from previously unthought-of efficiencies, but it also widely expands the number of possible threats a company faces.

Thus, the executive in the role of long-distance lookout should be scanning temporal, geographic, and relationship horizons for opportunities and threats. She will be looking for trends that are five or more years distant, for opportunities derived from fiscal, monetary, and diplomatic policies in other countries, and for threats that affect their customers' customers and their suppliers' suppliers. From this monitoring she will determine what metrics will confirm or deny trends or the thresholds that will dictate the proper time for a response. For instance, the long-distance lookout at a healthcare provider would see the aging trend noted by Greenspan and realize the potential impact of further strains on the Medicare system. Immediately, he might begin monitoring the nascent presidential campaigns for signs of policy positions on Medicare and Social Security. He might also draw other executives and the board's attention to the need to focus strategic efforts on providing geriatric care more efficiently, realizing the dual impact of government and insurance companies coming under extreme cost pressure and the demand for such services overwhelming provider resources. Alternatively, the long-distance lookout at a financial services firm will see the potential erosion of profits from a population that will be withdrawing far more assets than will be deposited or invested. She will recommend developing value-added services to advise senior citizens on stretching their retirement savings farther and will set up monitoring to determine whether the growth in services of this type offsets the profitability losses. A long-distance lookout at a residential construction company will see the need to move from homes designed for young or growing families (of which there will be a glut, as there will be far more empty-nesters trading down than young families looking for more bedrooms) to homes designed for older Americans. The long-distance lookout at a retailer will perceive the falling buying power of the young. Not only are they going to be outnumbered, but they will be competing for part-time jobs with retired people hoping to stretch their savings further; they will also find few promotion opportunities (and therefore few raises) because those ahead of them are no longer retiring.[11]

Recognizing these trends early will make all the difference in developing responses that will allow corporations to make smooth transitions from today's markets to tomorrow's. Companies that do will avoid the "abrupt and painful" changes that will humble many of today's largest companies who do not assign executives to take on the role of long-distance lookout.

Internal Monitor and Reporter

The new long-distance lookout function will appear first in organizations in two very different states: organizations that are succeeding and looking for ways to continue and expand and organizations that have suddenly lost a competitive edge or significant market share because they were caught unaware by an external market change that was off their radar screen. In companies struggling because of internal rather than external shocks, such as an earnings restatement, executive malfeasance or becoming the victim of a suspected event because information was not shared throughout the organization, a different new function will most likely emerge first. This new function will focus primarily on ensuring that corporate targets are measured accurately and reported truthfully to the rest of the organization, especially other senior executives and boards of directors.

The story of Sears's troubles in 2002 and the familiar stories of Enron, WorldCom, Tyco, Qwest, and others illustrate the information gap that all too frequently exists in corporations today. In each of these cases, vital information on corporate performance was not reported to the CEO or members of the board until far too late, if at all. These instances are just the tip of the iceberg. Every day managers confront difficult situations and create reports that put the best possible spin on negative information; frequently they can be less than forthcoming simply due to human nature. An outgrowth of the current climate of intolerance for even the slightest perception of misconduct (for example, the February 2003 dismissal of Sprint's CEO and president for using a tax shelter recommended and approved by the company's auditors and the fall 2003 scandal regarding executive pay and governance at the New York Stock Exchange[12]) will be the appointment of a senior executive to closely monitor corporate performance with an unbiased outlook and report on the performance to the relevant parties.

Perhaps the first company to appoint an executive to take on the function of internal monitor and reporter will be one that is emerging from bankruptcy. One of the little-known or publicized provisions of the U.S. bankruptcy code is the requirement that as companies are reorganizing under the protection of the code, they report progress toward their goals monthly. However, as soon as they emerge from bankruptcy, they are once again required to report on financial results only once every three months. Realizing the high priority of rebuilding investor confidence as an organization emerges from bankruptcy, in the not too distant future a reconstituted board and/or CEO will decide to continue the monthly reports, acknowledging the huge windfall of positive feeling such transparency will accrue. Of course, this prescient board will also recognize the imperative that this information be entirely correct (or that uncertain results be clearly identified).

Or perhaps the first executive assigned this function will be appointed by a board who has watched former senior executives paraded before television cameras in handcuffs in what is now commonly known as the "perp walk." This board may be less concerned with rebuilding the trust of the investing public than with protecting themselves from potential liability as officers of the corporation. They will want to ensure that they never again are the victims of false, misleading, or incomplete information provided to them by a CEO. This board may appoint an executive initially for the sole purpose of ensuring that they receive timely, complete, and accurate information. Corporate governance specialists are beginning to see the possibilities of the reporter/monitor function. Michael Useem, a professor at Wharton School of Business and currently serving as an advisor to Tyco as it struggles to emerge from the black cloud of scandal, has spoken in interviews of the need for an individual who has a "sacred duty" to ensure that the board of directors receives all the appropriate information.[13]

Of course, there will be other circumstances that drive the need for an internal monitor and reporter; circumstances that result from an organization's inability to distribute information widely. Whether or not these cases are grounded in a desire to cover up poor performance (like the origin of the Hayman fire) or simply a lack of understanding of the information needs of others, executive oversight to ensure that the "need-to-know" culture is overthrown and real-time information is distributed to everyone who needs it will be necessary. Many of the benefits of implementing real-time opportunity detection, such as Amberwood's ability to compete for out-of-state customers, are the result of sharing real-time information beyond the immediate confines of the process being monitored. An organization that does not ensure that information is shared across departments and across business units will leave a great deal of productivity and efficiency, a great deal of business benefit, sitting on the table and, of course, will continue to be unnecessarily vulnerable to suspected events.

To accomplish the task of ensuring that real-time information is monitored and reported to all the proper parties, the executive who takes on the function will need unprecedented power to travel throughout the organization in search of the data required for the reports that are mandated. The granting and use of this power will soon bring two additional and perhaps unanticipated duties to the function: (1) serving as the corporate FBI and (2) serving as the corporate "black box." As an internal monitor and reporter begins her task, she will sooner or later discover that some corporate goal or target is not being met. On reporting this information, the executive will often find herself tasked with determining exactly why the goal is not being achieved and with recommending specific courses of action to correct the problems perceived. Because of the already granted power to collect information throughout the organization, the executive who takes on this function will be the person best equipped to carry out the task. However, access to information will also make the holder of this position the repository for all vital corporate information whenever wrongdoing is alleged. This executive will probably find herself the first recipient of a subpoena when a criminal investigation is launched, a shareholder lawsuit is filed, or civil action is contemplated. Just as the black box is the first item investigators seek for determining the cause of an airplane accident, the internal monitor and reporter will be the first witness sought to determine the source of any wrongdoing. Indeed, as the role becomes more common, it is not out of the realm of possibility that internal monitors and reporters will be granted presumptive immunity from prosecution to increase the likelihood that they will proactively carry evidence of criminal activity to the appropriate authorities.

A New Corporate Officer?

The functions of change leader, lookout, and reporter will inevitably emerge as organizations travel the path to becoming Real-Time Enterprises; success in the endeavor requires at the least a Real-Time Enterprise change leader. As these functions emerge, organizations will face a critical choice: which executives will take on the functions?

There are immediate affinities between the "new" functions and the functions of existing senior management. CEOs, in the process of setting strategy are looking for emerging trends, COOs are charged with overseeing processes to ensure maximum efficiency, and CFOs are tasked with monitoring and reporting. In many organizations, the new functions will be formally or informally adopted by just these executives. In some organizations, only one or two of the new functions will emerge over the next five years. In others, all three are already in development.

Although the appropriation of these functions by existing executives seems efficient, it could perhaps be a disaster for effectiveness. Looking at these functions as extensions of the duties of existing executives misses the opportunity to design a new governance structure to maximize efficiency and effectiveness as the corporation makes the transition to being a Real-Time Enterprise. A new governance structure will involve the creation of a new executive officer of the corporation to take on all three of the functions, an executive we call the chief monitoring officer (CMO).

The appointment of a new officer responsible for these functions will maximize efficiency and effectiveness for three reasons: (1) existing officers simply do not have the time for additional duties; (2) even though it may not appear so at first glance, the functions are, in fact, distinct from the functions executives are currently tasked with; (3) the functions are complementary and would benefit from a single individual performing all of them.

New Functions Are in Addition to Existing Responsibilities

The day-to-day running of an organization does not permit the people in any of the existing C-level positions to give enough time and attention to items like global currency markets and Thai fiscal policy, the rapid aging of the developed world's population, and ensuring that the right processes are real-time enabled in the right order for maximum efficiency. The need for the CMO is grounded in the wisdom of Adam Smith and his classic work *The Wealth of Nations*, which formalized the concept of the division of labor. A new executive is needed in no small part to allow each of the existing executives to focus on what they do best: the CFO on financial management, the COO on operations, the CIO on technology management, and the CEO on bringing them all together and defining the strategic direction of the corporation. The CMO will benefit the corporation by single-mindedly focusing on the tasks described and these tasks alone, with the time to perform them as well as they need to be.

New Functions Are Distinct from Existing Responsibilities

It may seem odd to suggest a new corporate officer to take on functions that are related to the roles of existing officers. Isn't reporting the province of the chief financial officer and his staff? Isn't internal monitoring the job of the chief operating officer and her staff? Isn't one of the chief executive officer's primary roles to keep an eye on coming trends and prepare for them? The chief information officer's role is to ensure that the proper technology is deployed to meet business goals, isn't it?

The answer to all these questions is an unequivocal "Yes"; these senior executive positions exist for exactly these purposes. However, each of the new functions required by the Real-Time Enterprise of a chief monitoring officer is distinct from that traditionally assigned to the executive in question, and some parts of the functions are far beyond the duties of the other executives.

CEO

The CEO's role in setting corporate strategy will not be usurped in the least by the existence of a CMO who takes on the long-distance lookout function. In no way should the lookout function be interpreted as setting strategic direction; rather, the lookout function ensures that the CEO is aware of all internal and external factors that may affect the success of the strategies the CEO contemplates. Clearly, there is a need for CEOs to receive better intelligence on emerging opportunities and threats than they receive today. Aside from the examples in this book of

CEOs not being aware of vital information, CEOs, like all corporate employees, eventually suffer from blind spots incurred from living in the reality of daily corporate operations. How this situation results in well-run corporations suffering from disruptive technologies is described in Clayton Christensen's book *The Innovator's Dilemma*. Both the effects of disruptive technologies and unforeseen market, competitive, or macroeconomic shifts take CEOs with carefully planned strategies by surprise every day. For the sake of clarity, it's worth repeating that the long-distance lookout will be looking for signs of trouble or opportunity ahead but will not dictate the appropriate response; he will simply make recommendations. Just as the national security advisor does not dictate foreign policy to the president, a chief monitoring officer would not dictate responses to threats or opportunities to the CEO. In both cases, however, the executive will reject the opinions of the advisor at their peril.

CFO

The chief financial officer is typically involved in six major areas of activity: (1) financial strategy, (2) investment management (3) treasury management, (4) tax management, (5) cost planning and budgeting, and (6) financial operations.[14] CFOs would retain all these roles even if a CMO were appointed. In fact, a CMO's success in performing the internal monitoring and reporting function will depend in great measure on the effectiveness of the CFO and staff in performing their tasks and transforming them into real-time information flows. CFO staff members will oversee the process of identifying significant financial events and their transformation into continuously updated financial information streams. Particularly because members of the CFO's organization define the taxonomy of how a general ledger's revenue and expense categories will map to the major revenue, expense, asset, liability and equity accounts and categories found in internal and external financial reports, CMOs will rely on the CFOs to transform the process that turns business events (sales, salaries, purchases, and so on) into financial measures in real time. Specifically, CFOs will need to focus on moving away from the manual data collection and input efforts that prevail today. It does not matter if financial statements of account can be produced at a moment's notice if the information in the reports is not real-time.

The chief monitoring officer will rely on the CFO's financial reports and augment them by monitoring and reporting on nonfinancial metrics and measures. Few could argue with the need for expanding beyond financial measures to assess the true value and state of a company. The popularity of the Balanced Scorecard is testament enough to how much this need has been recognized. As many companies who have begun implementing the Balanced Scorecard or other operational frameworks like the European Foundation for Quality Management will tell you, there is nothing more critical than sustained management attention to ensure that the measures are accurate, appropriate, and most important, maintained over time. It is likely that some of the first CMOs will in fact be managers whose current role is to oversee the implementation and the ongoing use of an operations management framework. To summarize, the CMO will not take over the traditional financial management duties of the CFO; he will augment the financial reports with nonfinancial metrics from across the organization, as well as metrics used to monitor all relevant trends outside the corporation, and report them to the relevant parties (in real time, of course).

Some readers may also wonder how the CMO differs substantially from the independent auditors that companies must retain. Although there are a number of important distinctions, the primary difference is that auditors are tasked with evaluating, confirming, and reporting information about the past; the CMO will be exclusively devoted to evaluating, confirming, and reporting information about the present so that an organization can effectively engage in real-time opportunity detection.

COO

The difference between the chief operating officer and the proposed chief monitoring officer is one of control and scope. The COO, where the position exists, generally has control over all direct product (in the broadest sense of the word) creation processes. The CMO, in fulfilling the real-time change leader function, will not have direct control over any processes but rather will ensure that all processes, revenue generating or otherwise, are as efficient as possible and capable of generating the real-time information necessary for effective monitoring. Thus, the CMO will not directly change processes but will bring to the attention of the COO (and other officers) the processes that need attention. Additionally, appointing a CMO would help the CEO and other executives prioritize the improvement of processes across the organization, determining whether financial, sales, or production processes are the most crucial for updating for real time. The CMO's role will be particularly crucial in avoiding Braess's paradox—which describes how improving the speed of certain processes has the net effect of slowing the overall system[15]—as real-time improvements are made.

CIO

Finally, in contrast to the chief information officer, the chief monitoring officer will not become directly involved in technology decisions. The CMO will simply point to problems that require technological solutions and help define an enterprisewide view of the needs for real-time information. The CMO will help the corporation prioritize the problems with the greatest impact on the company's ability to monitor the appropriate metrics in real time.

New Functions Are Complementary to Each Other

Each of the new functions required by Real-Time Enterprises are complementary, meaning that they can be accomplished most efficiently when brought together in one person rather than dispersed to several different executives. Having different executives monitoring internal metrics and external threats (in the internal monitoring and reporting and long-distance lookout functions, respectively) would quickly lead to gaps and incomplete information. How can an assessment of external threats or opportunities be made without a thorough understanding of corporate capabilities? How can the soundness of internal operations be judged without an understanding of external market forces (for instance, one of the early warning signs of fraud at WorldCom was a capital cost structure very different from those of competitors)? Who better to oversee process changes than the executive who must rely on the information generated by the processes for internal monitoring and reporting? It simply makes sense to bring together internal and external monitoring and pair them with responsibility for ensuring that processes function as efficiently as possible.

It is impossible to say exactly how this new role may emerge in any particular organization, and in some it won't emerge at all. In some cases, the impetus will have more to do with corporate malfeasance than real-time information; in others it will be solely about real-time opportunity detection. Regardless of how the process starts, however, in most cases it will end with a new executive officer who takes all these functions.

Further Considerations for Chief Monitoring Officers

Questions regarding the need for another senior management position might include this one: "In today's economic environment, what company can afford to create and staff a whole new department?" Again the answer comes from examining the specific role the CMO will take on: Because the CMO will not have direct responsibility for any business process other than monitoring, the CMO should not have a department, and the number of direct reports of the effective CMO will be extremely small. In fact, managing a department will be anathema to successful chief monitoring officers since managing a large group of people would distract from the ability to monitor the far horizons for signs of coming disasters or opportunities. It could also create conflicts of interest (related to protecting a department or employees or other traditional signs of power and control) that would interfere with the CMO's primary responsibility to tell the truth, the whole truth and nothing but the truth to senior management and the board. The chief monitoring officer will primarily rely on the existing staff of other departments and on corporate shared services to gather the information she requires to provide warning and real-time reporting.

The Chief Monitoring Officer and the Board of Directors

The ultimate question is of corporate governance: To whom would the CMO report? Of course, different organizations will handle this issue differently; no two organizations have the exact same governance procedures. There is a compelling argument to be made, however, that maximum benefit will accrue to corporations that ensure the independence of their chief monitoring officer by having the CMO report only to the board of directors.

To explain this somewhat startling assertion, let's draw an analogy to the U.S. government, an institution seldom looked to for inspiration on solving business problems, particularly problems related to delays and bureaucracy.[16] The balance of power enshrined in the U.S. Constitution ensures that executive power is subject to the decisions of an independent group—the president can dictate policy with a great deal of latitude but ultimately depends on an independent group, the Congress, that approves the budget that allows the functioning of the apparatuses of government and can require or restrict certain policies. In a similar way, chief executives act with a great deal of independence but must secure approval from the nominally independent board of directors for budget allocations and strategy. U.S. history and corporate history both provide examples of the shifting balance of power between these two groups. At times, the executive is weak and closely controlled, at other times the Congress/board acts as a rubber stamp for the powerful executive. Unfortunately, on numerous occasions in U.S. politics, and frequently in the recent history of U.S. corporations, the executive has purposefully deceived the body that exists to enforce accountability. The U.S. Congress, unlike standard corporate governance schemes, has found a way to ensure that it has access to independent information about the performance of the government and internal and external factors that influence the health, welfare, and safety of the nation, allowing it to more effectively hold the executive branch accountable—the General Accounting Office (GAO). On its Web site (www.gao.gov), the GAO defines itself this way:

The General Accounting Office is the audit, evaluation, and investigative arm of Congress. GAO exists to support the Congress in meeting its Constitutional responsibilities and to help improve the performance and ensure the accountability of the federal government for the American people. GAO examines the use of public funds, evaluates federal programs and activities, and provides analyses, options, recommendations, and other assistance to help the Congress make effective oversight, policy, and funding decisions. In this context, GAO works to continuously improve the economy, efficiency, and effectiveness of the federal government through financial audits, program reviews and evaluations, analyses, legal opinions, investigations, and other services. GAO's activities are designed to ensure the executive branch's accountability to the Congress under the Constitution and the government's accountability to the American people. GAO is dedicated to good government through its commitment to the core values of accountability, integrity, and reliability.[17]

A better description of the role and purpose of the internal reporting and monitoring function of a chief monitoring officer would be difficult to write.

The key point here is that the GAO's independence from the executive branch is what allows it to objectively report on the efficiency and effectiveness of government. For chief monitoring officers to do the best possible job of warning the executives and the board, they must also be independent of the executive branch of the organization, the CEO. The testimony of Sherron Watkins of Enron before the House of Representative's Committee on Energy and Commerce in February 2002 illustrates this need: "I was not comfortable confronting Mr. Skilling or Mr. Fastow with my concerns. To do so, I believed, would have been a job-terminating move."[18] An effective CMO must have no concerns that reporting the true facts might endanger the job. Of course, Ms. Watkins's testimony also points to another of the potential benefits of having a CMO who reports to the board: the CMO would provide a safe haven for any employee to report suspicions of damaging or illegal behavior with little fear of reprisal. By having a CMO who reports to the board, a company would more than fulfill the whistleblower requirements of the Sarbanes-Oxley Act of 2002. Amid a vast collection of accounting and corporate governance related issues covered in the law is a provision protecting "whistleblowers" who fear their company "may discharge, demote, suspend, threaten, harass, or in any other manner discriminate" against them if they identify suspect or even illegal activities within the company.[19] The existence of an independent CMO will also serve as a powerful check on the first tentative steps toward fraud described by corporate bankruptcy and restructuring expert Greg Rayburn (see chapter 3). Michael Useem of Wharton and Tyco concurs:

> [Companies] need a mechanism to ensure that . . . information gets up to top management and the board. There are ample barriers to that, very well known and destructive in consequence as we've seen at some of the basket cases of the last two years. Therefore a person designated to unearth data, act as a contrarian, kick the tires, test the waters, whatever the metaphors might be, is a good idea.[20]

In fact, Useem states that having just one CMO at the executive level might not be enough; complete success may require multiple CMO-type positions spread throughout the organization. As he said in an interview with *Business Week*, "You have to have in place devices to guard against the evil that lurks within."[21] There is no better device to guard against temptation than an independent executive charged with always reporting the truth.

It should be noted, of course, that the GAO is not—nor will the CMO ever be—completely independent. The GAO depends on the Congress for its budget. In private conversations, GAO staffers will tell you that they are acutely aware of the strongly held opinions of some members of Congress who have a disproportionate influence on future budget requests of the

GAO. These GAO staffers' commitment to integrity is tested whenever they feel they must issue a report that does not support such a congressperson's opinion. The same will be the case for chief monitoring officers who will quickly become aware of the inclinations of various members of the board of directors. Complete independence is impossible, but having the CMO report to the board is the best way to ensure the most independence possible. Companies that grant their CMOs this level of independence will achieve maximum benefit from this new executive position.

No discussion on governance would be complete without a mention of compensation. Determining appropriate compensation schemes for chief monitoring officers will not be a trivial task. Experts will be challenged to develop new and innovative compensation schemes. One of the chief issues that will need to be addressed is the fact that the position of CMO, particularly if it assumes the internal monitoring and reporting function, will not be the best-loved position in the enterprise (see every movie and television show ever made that featured someone from a police department's internal affairs division). Without adequate remuneration to compensate for the potential for animosity, filling chief monitoring officer jobs will be significantly harder than filling seats on the board of directors is currently reputed to be.[22] Certainly the compensation of CMOs should be tied to corporate performance. However, evaluating a CMO's performance will not be a trivial task because the metrics of success for the position may not be immediately measurable. For CMOs who have the role of long-distance lookout, some sort of deferred compensation should probably be required. Determining appropriate compensation will not be easy, and for some companies working it out may delay the first CMO appointment or make it difficult to maintain anyone in the position for long.

Conclusion

The success of Real-Time Enterprises will rest in no small part on the successful incorporation of three new functions into the enterprise. Moving beyond real-time opportunity detection at the tactical level to steps 2 and 3 of becoming a Real-Time Enterprise requires three new functions. All business surprises won't end without a long-distance lookout; executives will not have all the information they need reported to them without an internal monitor and reporter; monitoring a company's most critical business processes and generating faster responses will not be possible without a Real-Time Enterprise change leader. Some organizations will travel the difficult path beyond real-time opportunity detection to becoming Real-Time Enterprises by assigning these functions to existing executives. The most successful Real-Time Enterprises, those that are praised, studied, and emulated, will combine these functions in a new senior executive, the chief monitoring officer. And in organizations that have the foresight to provide independence for the CMO, huge benefits will accrue. They will be the companies that dominate their markets a decade from now.

8

the future in a
real-time world

THE LAST TWO CHAPTERS have explored the changes
that applying real-time opportunity detection across an
organization will have on companies and their most important processes. The changes described are not, of
course, the only changes that will result. As more organizations equip themselves to consistently end surprises by
the systematic application of real-time opportunity detection and begin the process changes that will turn
them into Real-Time Enterprises, industries, economies,
and societies will be affected. Many of these changes
have little in common other than their source—more efficient and effective enterprises that are no longer the
victims of surprises.

Hype Cycle

To provide contexts and time frames for the changes that will occur, as well as to put the media hype about Real-Time Enterprises into context, it's helpful to map them to the Gartner Hype Cycle (figure 8-1). The Gartner Hype Cycle graphic has been used for years to illustrate the way a new technology or concept moves from inception to common use. It is remarkable that practically any technology or business innovation can be easily mapped to the stages of the Hype Cycle. Briefly, when a ground-breaking technology or concept is introduced (the trigger), it rapidly captures imaginations as individuals and groups begin to realize the potential applications. The popular press picks up on the idea and the stories written on the topic rapidly create a self-reinforcing explosion of expectation. Once the expectations reach their peak (the Peak of Inflated Expectations) and early adopters begin to encounter implementation challenges, articles begin to appear that question whether the new technology/idea is all it was promised to be (and of course it never is since by this point expectations are far higher than could

FIGURE 8-1

The hype cycle shows how new technologies or business concepts are adopted.

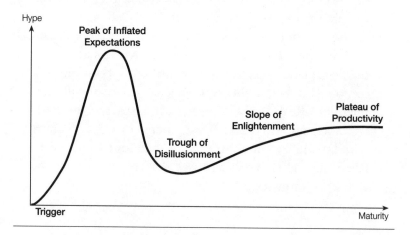

possibly be met). Expectations fall rapidly, and in a short time the conventional wisdom dramatically shifts from irrationally praising the new technology/idea to irrationally criticizing it (the Trough of Disillusionment). Finally, in the background, companies who had implemented the new idea/technology when it first emerged begin showing benefits (the Slope of Enlightenment). Slowly but surely, a new consensus emerges that while the new technology/idea is not the solution to all problems, it is the solution to some (the Plateau of Productivity). This trajectory has recently been followed by concepts like the Balanced Scorecard and customer relationship management and by technologies like wireless local area networks, all of which are now emerging as real business tools with realistic expectations of their use and impact.

Real-time opportunity detection—more specifically, the Real-Time Enterprise concept—will follow a similar trajectory, which is mapped out in figure 8-2. Today, we are approaching the Peak of Inflated Expectations, with magazine cover stories and more than 10,000 articles available with a single Google search.

FIGURE 8-2

This aggressive Real-Time Enterprise hype cycle shows important milestones as an RTE develops.

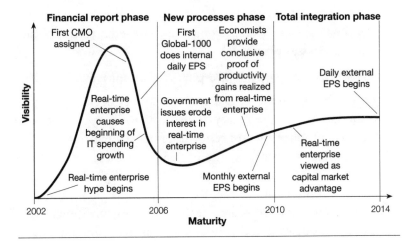

(One key sign the Plateau of Productivity has been reached is when vendors and consultants adopt a concept as a veneer on top of whatever products they had already been selling.) Underneath the rise and fall of hype about Real-Time Enterprise, progress (as shown in the examples in chapters 5 and 6) is being made in many companies as they implement real-time opportunity detection. The result, independent of the rise and fall of public attention, will be profound changes in the culture and processes of individual businesses and the economy as a whole. The Real-Time Enterprise Hype Cycle is admittedly aggressive in its timing, but it provides a framework for understanding the general sequence of changes that will be wrought by Real-Time Enterprises.

At this point, it is worth noting two things:

1. The timelines of different organizations may be vastly different; some organizations will be delivering daily earnings per share reports to the CEO and CFO while others are still unfamiliar with the concepts of the Real-Time Enterprise.

2. There is no timeline for the steps within an organization—the appointment of a CMO does not inevitably lead to the next change within a specific amount of time. Some organizations will move through the changes quickly, others very slowly, and neither necessarily in the order presented here (GM, for example, has skipped parts of the financial reporting phase and moved directly to the new processes phase).

The development of Real-Time Enterprises will fall into three general phases. In the first, as senior executives decide to commit resources to the necessary transformations, organizations will focus on monitoring and reporting financial metrics such as revenue, expenses, cash flow, and earnings. As these metrics are transformed, inefficient processes will be highlighted, kicking off the second phase of change, the new process phase. Finally, after inefficient processes are dealt with, organizations will begin looking outward and connecting their real-time information flows with partners, both customers and suppliers, ushering in the total integration phase.

Many of the changes and milestones along the way to becoming a Real-Time Enterprise will be expected. However, additional changes, both positive and negative, to the environment inside corporations as well as in the entire economy may be entirely unexpected.

Financial Reporting Phase

As the examples in chapters 5 and 6 show, some companies have already entered the financial reporting phase. Leaders in every industry will be entering and often completing this phase by 2006.

Real-Time Earnings per Share for Executives

Among the first measurable results of the drive toward becoming a Real-Time Enterprise will be the creation of daily financial reports for executives. A 2001 survey conducted by PricewaterhouseCoopers[1] on behalf of the World Economic Forum asked 1,161 CEOs, "[What] do you take into account/do investors take into account when assessing company value?" Unsurprisingly, the most popular answers were earnings and cash flow (figure 8-3).

As a result, when CEOs and their management teams take on the task of becoming a Real-Time Enterprise and implement the Identification Model, the answer to the initial questions of goals and priorities posed by the model is likely to be the earnings and cash flow metrics. And of course, these two metrics would easily pass through the rest of the Identification Model and sail through the Justification Model. Once senior management starts on the course of real-time opportunity detection, earnings and cash flow will be two of the first metrics to be tracked; they will be monitored in the form of daily earnings per share reports distributed internally.

A number of organizations are already close. Michael Relich, CIO at Wet Seal, says that his organization's focus on gathering real-time sales data has already put them close to being able to

FIGURE 8-3

PricewaterhouseCoopers CEO survey indicates that the prime concerns of CEOs are cash flow and earnings.

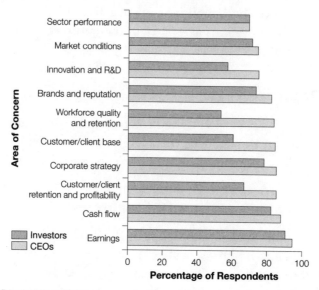

Source: PricewaterhouseCoopers.

accurately estimate earnings from operations on a daily basis. Key to this ability is the fact that retail sales personnel use the point-of-sale systems to "clock in." Using this technology enabler, Wet Seal is capturing the major portion of variable personnel expenses simultaneously with sales. Relich comments that, while daily earnings are not a goal the company has yet focused on, "the major difficulty would be ensuring that the folks at headquarters are inputting purchase orders in real time. We have all the data we need from the stores to do it."[2] One large services company with very stable fixed costs (the company asked not to be named) has been analyzing its customer profiles and correlating customer types with revenue. With more than three years of collected data, the company can now predict the present revenue generated by customers based on real-time information on the number of customers of each type at the beginning of a quarter. With that information, it can determine within a 1 percent margin of error what earnings will be at the end of the quarter.

Impact on IT Spending and the Economy

Perhaps the first broadly noticed impact of companies becoming Real-Time Enterprises will be growth in IT spending. The process and IT challenges to becoming a Real-Time Enterprise will not only serve as drivers for the emergence of chief monitoring officers, they will kick off the first significant growth in IT spending since the dot-com craze. Following are some of the primary focus areas of this spending.

- Integrating the data that already exist in customer data records, enterprise resource planning systems, logistics systems, risk management systems, accounting systems, and others (business example: Dresdner Kleinwort Wasserstein)

- Automatically capturing data that today require manual processes (business example: Amberwood Homes)

- Creating networks to distribute data in real time to geographically distributed recipients (business example: Wet Seal)

- Providing real-time analytic tools that will allow managers to mine the data in search of unexpected results and their causes (for example, the systems that would have benefited the airline industry)

Replacing inefficient manual processes with technology as well as upgrading existing systems for handling real-time information will be a major boon to the IT industry. The growth in IT spending will have larger implications as well. An examination of the most recent recession reveals how important IT spending is to the overall state of the economy.

Of course, the productivity benefits of Real-Time Enterprises will provide an even greater benefit to the economy and pave the way for more technology investments to continue the drive toward real-time monitoring of all relevant metrics.

from real-time opportunity detection to real-time enterprise

AN IT-LED RECESSION FOLLOWED BY AN IT-LED RECOVERY?

The recession that began in March 2001 was somewhat peculiar. A recession requires shrinking gross domestic product for two consecutive quarters, but in March 2001 only one of the three components of GDP was falling. Consumer spending was actually on the rise, and government consumption was at least level. The only portion of GDP that fell was gross private domestic investment (figure 8-4). Within this measure, the biggest decline was in business capital spending. Drilling down another level shows that the major cause of the decline of business capital investments was a dramatic fall in IT investments (figure 8-5).[3]

Therefore, as IT investments grow to enable Real-Time Enterprises, the overall economy will receive a significant boost.

FIGURE 8-4

Elements of gross domestic product show that only gross private domestic investment fell during the last recession.

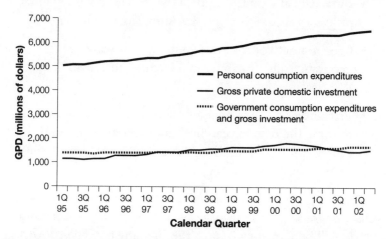

Source: Bureau of Economic Analysis, U.S. Department of Commerce, "Summary of Percent Change from Preceding Period in Real Gross Domestic Product and Related Measures," National Income and Products Accounts, 30 May 2003. Available at <http://www.bea.gov/bea/dn/nipaweb/SelectTable.asp?Popular=Y> (accessed 10 June 2003).

FIGURE 8-5

**Elements of nonresidential fixed investment from 1995
through 2002 show that the decline in IT spending was
primarily responsible for the economic downturn.**

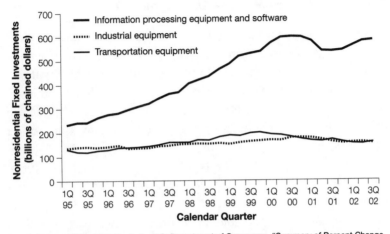

Source: Bureau of Economic Analysis, U.S. Department of Commerce, "Summary of Percent Change
from Preceding Period in Real Gross Domestic Product and Related Measures," National Income and
Products Accounts, 30 May 2003. Available at <http://www.bea.gov/bea/dn/nipaweb/SelectTable.
asp?Popular=Y> (accessed 10 June 2003).

Balancing this positive impact somewhat will be job losses related to the gains in productivity enabled by the spending on information technology. As technology is used to replace manual
processes for capturing information in real time, a category of
workers will no longer be necessary. The jobs lost will primarily
be jobs that were created by the deployment of nonintegrated
systems that therefore required human beings to take data from
one process or system and transfer them to another.

New Processes Phase

Industry-leading companies that have implemented new real-
time financial reporting will soon turn their attention to the
process delays they had to overcome to generate real-time earnings per share information for their executives. As in the financial reporting phase, once the new processes phase is begun,

there will be job losses, this time at every rung of the corporate ladder, as the focus moves from data collection to improving the efficiency of responses.

Governance Challenges—The Short-Term CEO

In the last chapter we mentioned the people challenges that will be faced as organizations make the transition to real-time processes. Michael Relich, CIO of Wet Seal, recalls his first foray into real-time information at a now defunct retailer. "Managers became so hung up on looking at the most recent transaction that they lost sight of the big picture. They were making poorer decisions, not better decisions, with the information."[4] Managers and executives at all levels will struggle with the transition, and these struggles will lead, in some companies, to management and governance disasters.

For some time there has been much criticism, referred to earlier in the book, of the singular focus today's capital markets place on meeting quarterly earnings expectations. Many complain that the net result is CEOs who lose sight of the long term and manage exclusively quarter to quarter. The reason for complaint, of course, is that while this myopia may maximize short-term results, it spells ruin in the long term. As the concept of the Real-Time Enterprise begins its slide from the heights of inflated expectations, this will be one of the primary charges leveled against it—real time information on earnings and cash flow accentuates the short-term view where it already existed and creates it in situations where it previously had not existed.

This charge will have evidence to back it up. Chief executives will be as vulnerable as other managers to the misuse and misinterpretation of real-time information. One scenario that will emerge is the chief executive deciding that only executives who directly contribute to earnings and cash flow will be direct reports. As a result, senior managers from chief information officers and corporate counsel to human resources managers and chief financial officers will find themselves demoted in terms of the reporting hierarchy. Another scenario will see some chief executives become micromanagers in the extreme. These CEOs will fall prey to the same disease that Michael Relich cited—they will chase down any item that doesn't meet expectations, no matter how small. The situation will be similar to the one many of us experienced the first time we had access to real-time information on stock prices on our computers. It was incredibly tempting to simply watch the numbers as they ticked up and down. Soon we found ourselves trying to identify the cause of any minor change: "Was there a press release? Did a competitor just announce earnings? Has a new Fed report been issued?" A situation like this has already occurred at Maxtor, a disk-drive maker. When executives were first supplied with real-time data on inventory levels and sales backlogs, they spent a great deal of time arguing over which numbers were the most current.[5] Even though these are simplistic examples, it's easy to see how some executives will be trapped by real-time information, obsessively monitoring each new change in financial metrics and focusing on it to the detriment of the overall business. Just as a driver who focuses all her attention on the speedometer to ensure that the right speed is maintained puts herself in jeopardy by not watching the road, so the good intentions of these executives will lead to the negative outcomes they are trying to prevent.

There will, of course, be other governance challenges. The chief monitoring officer (or the roles the CMO encompasses) will not fit in smoothly in many organizations. In some there will be a major battle among executives and their boards over whether, in fact, there will be a CMO and which executives will report to the board of directors. In other companies, the chief operating officer and the chief financial officer will feel that their authority has been usurped by the chief monitoring officer, and they will rebel, either by resigning or causing considerable difficulty in the executive suite. As experience shows, companies that have these difficulties will struggle in relation to competitors. There will be news stories that correlate Real-Time Enterprises to executive turnover or determine from the struggles of a company fighting internal governance battles that there is no value in becoming a Real-Time Enterprise. These situations will not predominate, but they will exist and they will be publicized, causing some to delay real-time projects or abandon them altogether.

Meanwhile, in the background, governance issues will be resolved in some organizations, which will begin to experience further benefits from Real-Time Enterprise transformation. Many CEOs will see real-time information on earnings and cash flow much as pilots view the traffic collision avoidance systems on their airplanes. Because the pilots are confident that they will be alerted of any impending danger of a collision, they can focus their attention on other important matters rather than constantly monitoring the radar for the approach of other airplanes. These executives will distribute real-time information widely and trust their teams to respond appropriately when real-time earnings and cash flow information reveals a problem or to notify them when (and only when) the attention of the chief executive is required.

This is the approach taken by Rick Wagoner at GM. Despite all GM's measurements of real-time production data, Wagoner is alerted, by his estimate, less than once a month when a problem requires his attention. CEOs like Wagoner will not micromanage, but they will avoid bureaucracy and go directly to the source when they perceive a problem that needs to be resolved quickly. As a result, a far larger number of managers and employees will become used to answering questions posed directly by their chief executive as she seeks out the source of a problem and the appropriate response. GM sales executives, for instance, know that whenever sales are below forecast for three days in a row, they will receive a phone call from Wagoner inquiring about their plans to bring sales back in line.

Chief executives who, like Rick Wagoner, use real-time information as a tool to free themselves from daily operations that do not require their attention will quickly see an increase in the amount of time they have to devote to strategic planning. So becoming a Real-Time Enterprise need not exacerbate problems of overattention to short-term goals; just the opposite—it can allow far more focus on long-term planning.

The *Titanic Syndrome*

The story of the sinking of the *Titanic* is rich with lessons about the value and use of real-time information. The story of the *Ti-*

REAL-TIME MARKETING

As real-time information on sales, cash flow, and earnings is developed, it is not only the roles of CEOs and CFOs that will be affected. Another area that will see profound changes is marketing. Few marketing-related activities stand to benefit more from real-time monitoring than the practice of "closed loop" marketing. In this scenario, drawing on information stored in a corporate data warehouse, a company can devise an advertising campaign designed to attract a specific target audience. Once the advertising campaign is underway, data can be collected from selected members of the target audience to gauge their receptiveness to the offering. As a result of the real-time feedback from the target group, modifications to the offering are made rapidly to maximize its success. Once modifications have been introduced, the process continues with further monitoring of reactions, further modifications from customer feedback, and so on.

The immediate feedback on marketing programs that will be possible in Real-Time Enterprises will be both a blessing and a curse to marketing professionals. Real-time sales feedback will allow marketers to finetune campaigns focused on immediate sales goals to achieve the exact results desired. On the other hand, the clear return on investment for short-term campaigns will put enormous pressure on marketers to determine metrics for showing return on campaigns focused on long-term goals, such as branding and brand awareness. With real-time feedback on results, marketing professionals will be tested as never before to show direct and specific results from marketing efforts.

tanic also holds an instructive lesson about hubris on the road to Real-Time Enterprises. One of the major blows to the public perception of Real-Time Enterprises during their development over the next ten years will be a *Titanic*-type disaster at an organization that claims to be a Real-Time Enterprise. As is commonly known, the *Titanic* was dubbed "unsinkable" when she was built, and the faith in her invulnerability led directly to the disaster that occurred. Despite warnings about the presence of icebergs in the waters in which the ship was traveling, the captain, fearful of any delays on the maiden voyage, trusted in the integrity of his vessel and proceeded at full speed, creating a situation where a sudden change in course, when it was required, was not possible.

The bottom of the Trough of Disillusionment with Real-Time Enterprises will likely be reached when a Fortune 1000 company learns the wrong lessons from its success with real-time opportunity detection. This self-declared Real-Time Enterprise will conclude that it has determined every factor that needs to be monitored and will proceed full speed ahead with its strategic plans. The company will neglect sound risk management practices, believing them to be obsolete. As a result, it will be taken completely off guard by a market shift it is not monitoring and will suffer huge losses to revenue, market share, and share price, bringing temporary ignominy to Real-Time Enterprise development. However, just as the *Titanic* disaster did not spell the end of transatlantic travel, this disaster will not spell the end of Real-Time Enterprises. In fact, many, seeing that there was warning before the disaster, will ultimately conclude that the disaster is the proof of the benefits of Real-Time Enterprises. The companies that reach this conclusion will redouble their efforts to ensure that they are monitoring both events and risk management positions and honing their abilities to respond. Many companies that have not yet appointed chief monitoring officers will do so immediately to ensure that they do not overlook critical data in their Real-Time Enterprise deployments.

Preferred Customer and Supplier Status

Real-Time Enterprise deployments will also have a dramatic impact on creation and maintenance of networks of suppliers and customers similar to the effect of Wal-Mart's transformation of retail networks. Wal-Mart has come to dominate both the retailing space and stories of business best practices. Not only is it the world's largest company in revenue, at over $250 billion in 2002, and the employer of one of every twenty retail workers in the United States, but case studies of how the company does everything from hiring to inventory management to negotiation to IT implementations can be regularly found in books and magazines. One of these stories, perhaps apocryphal, perhaps not, tells of a sign in the conference room in Bentonville, Arkansas, where the company meets with potential new suppliers. The sign is reputed to warn those who are interested in doing business with Wal-Mart that unless they are capable of electronically exchanging inventory and purchasing information using Wal-Mart's systems they shouldn't bother to stay for the meeting. One of the cornerstones of Wal-Mart's success is its use of technology to manage inventories far better than its competitors. Thus, Wal-Mart refuses to do business with suppliers that cannot conform to its inventory management systems.

In a similar way, as more and more companies develop into Real-Time Enterprises, they will realize the substantial efficiency and productivity benefits to be realized when they deal with companies with a similar ability to predict the present. These will be the partners most likely to share information with each other, enabling all involved to monitor events earlier in the event–impact chain and therefore be immune to surprises. As customers, Real-Time Enterprises will be able to commit to volumes of purchases farther into the future and will be able to honor their commitments better than others. As suppliers, Real-Time Enterprises will be able to guarantee prices and availability farther into the future than others. In both cases, the stability and predictability of the partners will reduce risk. Therefore, organizations will offer preferred terms to and compete harder for the business of other Real-Time Enterprises.

Dan Johnson of Amberwood Homes has already seen the beginning of this preferential option for Real-Time Enterprises. Amberwood's real-time scheduling allows subcontractors to see what jobs they are scheduled for six months in advance. This allows them to cut inventories since they do not have to be prepared for a surprise call to a job. Johnson believes that in less than five years, fully half the builders in the Phoenix area will be using similar real-time scheduling. "When that happens," he says, "the subcontractors will quickly start charging builders who aren't using real-time scheduling more. It just doesn't make sense for them not to—doing business without these schedules is more expensive for the subcontractors."[6] Just as doing business with suppliers who cannot trade information electronically is too expensive for Wal-Mart to accept, so too will doing business with non-Real-Time Enterprises become for many organizations.

Impact on Boards of Directors

Internal relationships and governance will also be affected by the growing use of real-time opportunity detection. We've already discussed some of the governance changes that will be necessary to achieve Real-Time Enterprise success. Other unforeseen changes in governance will come about, particularly for boards of directors.

Any discussion of the role of the boards of directors of U.S.-based companies must start with the incorporation laws of Delaware, under which more than half of U.S. public companies are incorporated. Delaware corporate law requires that "the business and affairs of every corporation organized under this chapter shall be managed by or under the direction of a board of directors" who are responsible for "appoint[ing] such officers and agents as the business of the corporation requires."[7] The board, of course, is not absolved of its fiduciary duties simply by appointing officers. The state courts of Delaware have established that the fulfillment of the fiduciary duties can be measured based on three criteria: due care, good faith, and loyalty.[8] Directors must fulfill their obligation of "care" by informing themselves on matters pertaining to the company, especially on issues affecting decisions.[9]

Recent events involving accounting scandals, "sudden" bankruptcies, departing CEOs, and plummeting stock prices would seem to indicate that many boards have fallen considerably short of meeting the standard of due care. Indeed, this is one reason why the directors of companies who have experienced such scandals tend to claim that they were deceived by executives. Delaware law absolves directors from responsibility for independently verifying information they receive from the officers they have appointed, stating that directors shall be "fully protected in relying in good faith upon the records of the corporation and upon such information, opinions, reports or statements presented to the corporation by any of the corporation's officers or employees."[10] Many independent observers have noted that one of the current problems with boards' oversight is that the board members are typically fully employed, often as the CEOs of other companies, and are unable or unwilling to spend the amount of time required to exercise due care.

The emergence of Real-Time Enterprises and especially of chief monitoring officers will obviously benefit board members as they attempt to meet their fiduciary duties, but it may have some darker implications as well.[11] On the positive side, the availability of real-time information on the most important aspects of corporate performance will give directors more and better insight into the true state of the corporation they are charged with overseeing, without significantly more effort or time on their part. The more information that is distributed to the board, the greater the transparency of the company's operations, the harder it will be to hide or obscure any negative information or unethical dealings.

On the other hand, once real-time information on the most important corporate performance measures is made available and/or a CMO is appointed, it is possible that a director's increased awareness of potential problems will introduce new risk, exposure, and increased liability if the company falters or fails, despite the early warnings it receives from real-time monitoring of critical business processes. The directors will never again be able to have "plausible deniability" of their knowledge of corporate affairs. Any announcement by the company of missed expectations, revenues falling faster than industry average, or risk mismanagement will expose the board to a greater degree of potential liability. If the board was receiving real-time information that showed the company's trajectory, shareholders could argue that the board did not exhibit due care, good faith, or loyalty by not acting to correct the problem. It's not inconceivable that a shareholder lawsuit in such a case would fault the board for not seeking or exercising more oversight of operations. The exposure may be greater, though, for boards that do not mandate that real-time information on progress toward goals be presented at each board meeting (or who do not appoint a chief monitoring officer), particularly if another firm in their industry has done so. In these cases, the first hint of bad news will certainly bring shareholder suits claiming that the simple fact that the board had not yet appointed a chief monitoring officer or demanded real-time operational information is evidence of a lack of due care. Regardless, Real-Time Enterprises and chief monitoring officers will present new practice opportunities for law firms, whether they represent disgruntled investors or defend companies.

These possibilities will wreak havoc for a time in the directors' and officers' liability insurance market (known as D&O). D&O insurance provides a company and its directors and officers with protection against losses caused by unfavorable court decisions, or where legal indemnification of directors and officers is limited or nonexistent.[12] An example of this kind of protection would be a court's finding that "wrongful acts" were committed by a company's directors or officers.[13] Delaware and other state courts place a heavy burden of proof on the plaintiffs in wrongful act suits, but it will not be known what effect having real-time information and the presence or absence of a chief monitoring officer will have until a number of cases are litigated. It is likely that insurance companies in the D&O market will hedge their risks by raising the premiums for all companies or even refusing to write new policies until the risks are better understood.

Ultimately, Real-Time Enterprises will find it easier to attract quality board members simply because of the greater level of transparency. The "market" for high-quality board members will follow a similar path to that of relationships between companies and their suppliers—only Real-Time Enterprises need apply. Although there will be ups and downs while the liability implications are sorted out, companies will discover that they cannot attract the quality of candidates they would like for their boards unless they are Real-Time Enterprises.

Total Integration Phase

Unsurprisingly, as more and more companies adopt Real-Time Enterprise processes and begin connecting themselves to other

Real-Time Enterprises, they will begin having a significant impact on the overall economy. We do not expect there to be a sufficient volume of companies operating as Real-Time Enterprises for the effects to be felt until after 2010, but the impact will be dramatic when it comes.

Managing the Macroeconomy

The National Bureau of Economic Research is responsible for officially documenting business cycles in the U.S. economy. The NBER determines when a recession or an expansion starts and ends. One of the more recent announcements by the NBER was its determination that a recession began in March of 2001.[14] The announcement, however, did not occur until November 26, 2001, eight months after the recession began! Even more shocking is the July 17, 2003, announcement that the recession ended at about the same time the announcement of its beginning was made—the announcement coming this time eighteen months after the event. These are not abnormal delays. Table 8-1 shows the lag time of all of the NBER's business cycle announcements for the past twenty-five years.

TABLE 8-1

Delays in NBER Declarations on the Business Cycle

Start date of economic cycle event	Lag between start date of economic cycle event and date of NBER's declaration
November 2001 trough	18 months
March 2001 peak	8 months
March 1991 trough	19 months
July 1990 peak	9 months
November 1982 trough	8 months
July 1981 peak	5 months
July 1980 trough	12 months
January 1980 peak	6 months

These gaps between the event of falling gross domestic product and its announcement would be trivial if the announcements were purely an academic exercise, but of course they are not. Monetary and fiscal policies all over the world are influenced by the state of the U.S. economy, not least the policies of the Federal Reserve Bank. Given the lag in definitively reporting the state of the GDP, it is fair to ask, "If the Federal Reserve had had this information as it occurred, would its board have reduced interest rates sooner or more aggressively during the 2001 downturn?"

Of course, the Federal Reserve does not rely solely on NBER declarations to determine its monetary policy positions. The Fed's economists rely on a vast array of data sources to mold its final decisions, including the Conference Board's Leading Economic Indicators, labor statistics, the Consumer and Producer Price Indexes, and so on. These measures however are also far from real-time measures.

Figure 8-6 shows six economic measurements that are used to help determine the health of the overall economy, along with the time between the end of a measured period and when the results for the period are disclosed. As you can see, it takes ten days after the end of a month for the Department of Labor to

FIGURE 8-6

By the time data is collected by the U.S. Departments of Labor and Commerce and delivered to fiscal and monetary policy planners, the data is painfully out of date.

report on the employment status of the nation. It takes the Department of Commerce a full three months after the end of a quarter to provide the final economic performance results for that quarter. Additionally, the initial numbers provided are often revised several times so that, for instance, the final numbers for the first, second, and third quarters of 2001 were not announced until July 31, 2002, a gap of 487, 396, and 304 days, respectively.[15]

There are many reasons why so much time is required to gather individual economic measurements. Days are required to compile information from thousands of enterprises polled by the Department of Labor to generate the nation's labor reports, while weeks and months are required to finalize foreign trade and business inventory statistics before final GDP results are released by the Department of Commerce. As more and more of the individual companies that provide the data for these economic reports become Real-Time Enterprises, however, the capability to gather the data required for the reports in real time will grow as well. As the economic reports move closer to reporting events in real time, fiscal and monetary policy will begin enjoying the same opportunities as individual Real-Time Enterprises. No longer will the Federal Reserve Board wait for three to six months after an interest rate increase or decrease to determine its effectiveness—the state of the GDP, consumer spending, business investment, and employment will be monitored daily. Just as managers are making better decisions as they predict the present, so too will the secretary of the Treasury, Congress, and the president be making better decisions with real-time information on the economy. In this manner, Real-Time Enterprises will further stabilize national economies as they enable fiscal and monetary policy makers to finetune their actions to diminish the harmful effects of an economic downturn while hastening the arrival of an economic recovery.

Daily Earnings per Share

Another mechanism made possible by Real-Time Enterprise deployments, daily earnings per share, will work in conjunction with policy makers' improved insight to help smooth economic cycles by taking much of the surprise out of stock markets. In the United States, section 13 of the Securities and Exchange Act of 1934 sets the rules for disclosure of financial information by public companies. Any company with more than $10 million in assets and more than five hundred shareholders must file periodic reports on the state of the company and its finances. Specifically, regular quarterly reports (Form 10Q) and annual reports (Form 10K) must be filed.[16] And reports on extraordinary events that occur, such as a bankruptcy filing, the resignation of an officer or a director, or a change in control of the corporation (Forms 8-K and 8-B) must also be filed.[17]

The intent of the rules is to protect investors by requiring the disclosure of material information about the performance of companies in which they are or are considering becoming shareholders. In today's world these rules hardly provide any protection at all, and it's not because of the willful manipulation of the reports by some criminal executives. The rules provide little protection because the law has not been updated significantly since 1934 to recognize the speed of today's capital markets, where an afternoon announcement in Tokyo can dramatically affect the outlook of a U.S. company and its stock price well before anyone on the East Coast of the United States is awake.

Under today's securities laws, quarterly reports for the first three quarters of the fiscal year are not due until 45 days after the end of the quarter and the combined fourth-quarter and annual report is not due until ninety days after the end of the fiscal year.[18] This means that an investor must wait up to 137 days from the start of the first three quarters before receiving any information about performance in that quarter and up to 182 days from the start of the fourth fiscal quarter before receiving any information about the company's performance. Even an extraordinary event like a filing for bankruptcy need not be disclosed for 15 days after it has occurred. While investors have access to real-time data on stock prices, in a bitter irony, the information the stock prices are based on is nearly ready to be archived by the time it is released.

Custom and practice have served to bring about more frequent unofficial disclosures (for instance, companies most often

issue a press release on earnings before filing their reports with the SEC), but the scale of this change is miniscule, closing the gap between business events and reports by a few days rather than weeks or months. On the regulatory front, recent changes, such as Regulation Full Disclosure, which requires that all released information be available to the entire public simultaneously, and the Sarbanes-Oxley Act, have actually discouraged executives from releasing information on performance more frequently. Even the attempts to specifically address the massive information time lag are minor; an example is this 2002 proposal from the SEC:

> The Commission intends to propose that public companies file their annual reports on Form 10-K within 60 days after the end of their fiscal year, rather than 90 days. The Commission also intends to propose that public companies file their quarterly reports on Form 10-Q within 30 days after the end of their first three fiscal quarters, rather than 45 days.[19]

Change will come to the way public companies report financial results but this change will be led by Real-Time Enterprises, not by regulations. As discussed, one of the first efforts of companies attempting to transform themselves will be to gain real-time financial performance information, with the particular goal being the common measure of a public company's success, earnings per share. Many companies will be approximating or even exactly determining this number by the latter half of the decade and reporting it to senior executives and board members. As executives adopt the changes in business processes and procedures brought about by real-time monitoring, they will have unprecedented insight into the operational and financial performance of their companies. Why not share some of the information with investors to enable them to determine the empirical soundness of the company more frequently than just four times per year? As we reach the end of the decade, a chief executive at some corporation that is generating daily earnings per share information internally and succeeding relative to its competition will determine that he can gain significant advantages in capital markets by announcing audited financial results not only within twenty-four to forty-eight hours after the end of a quarter, but more important, at specific intervals within the quarter, for instance monthly. Investors will undoubtedly flock in droves to a successful company with this level of transparency and currency of information.

The day of the first announcement of monthly earnings per share, regardless of whether the executive realizes it or not, will be a cousin to July 16, 1945, the day the first atomic bomb was exploded. Just as the successful detonation of the first atomic device at Alamogordo, Nevada, unleashed a nuclear arms race that dominated the politics of the next fifty years, the first voluntary announcement of near real-time earnings will mark the start of a financial "arms race" that will dominate financial markets for years. Immediately after the first announcement, other companies in the same industry will be forced by the market to provide the same level of transparency.[20] Additionally, companies in other industries will note the capital market success achieved by this first mover and attempt to replicate it. Soon, another organization will raise the stakes by announcing weekly reports. From there, it will only be a few short ideological steps (though taken over a matter of years) to daily reporting of financial results.

Effect on Capital Markets

Finally, as daily and weekly reporting and improved ability for macroeconomic management come together, major shifts in international capital flows may occur. If one area of the industrialized world significantly outpaces others in these changes, there will be a steady flow of capital out of laggard economies and into those where the use of real-time information has produced more stable economies, more predictable growth, and fewer surprises. The achievement of these results will not require all or even a majority of companies to successfully navigate the path to becoming Real-Time Enterprises. Once 20 to 30 percent of companies have made significant progress toward eliminating business surprises, they will exert a stabilizing influence on the economy disproportionate to their size. Because they will neither overcommit in changing markets nor miss valuable opportunities, these organizations will help smooth out business cycles protecting non-Real-Time Enterprises from sudden market shifts.

An argument can be made that this scenario of a steady shift in capital from one or more regions to another is likely to favor the United States at the expense of Japan and Europe. If historical trends hold, then Europe's slower adoption of technology will limit progress there while Japan's suspicions of transparency and structural change may prove an impediment in that country. On the other hand, the companies of South Korea and Singapore that have actively and enthusiastically embraced technology may provide a boost for those economies. Clearly, there will be exceptions; individual companies all over the globe will emerge as Real-Time Enterprise leaders. The globalized nature of the world economy may balance out the historical tendencies of various countries and regions. However, if they do not, policy action may be required in countries that have fallen behind to force rapid change to limit the impact of capital shifts.

Conclusion

A little change, when it is of the Real-Time Enterprise variety, goes a long way. Beginning with individual managers who predict the present and give themselves and their superiors a heads-up to challenges and opportunities, sweeping changes will be set in motion. These changes, as they spread, will change the way companies are governed, the way companies choose suppliers and customers, and the way national economies are managed and compete in the global economy. These changes will occur gradually over the next ten to twenty years, sometimes over-hyped and sometimes entirely ignored as media and managers climb the Peak of Inflated Expectations and crash into the Trough of Disillusionment. Ultimately, these changes will occur and will be recognized as the final results of the end of business surprises brought about real-time opportunity detection.

conclusion:
the time is now

HIS BOOK BEGAN with the rather startling assertion that there is always warning of business disasters and opportunities and, more important, that individual managers today, for the first time in history, have the capability to end business surprises as we know them. The tools to do so are either in place or commonly available. The only impediments are the false assumptions that business surprises cannot be stopped. Wet Seal, Ford, eBay, and others are proving the old assumptions false every day. Ever larger parts of their businesses are becoming invulnerable to surprises because they are tracking material information about their most important goals in real time (and not getting lost in a mountain of real-time data on nonmaterial issues). The diversity of these companies shows that the principles of predicting the present and real-time opportunity detection are not limited to certain industries or companies of a particular size. Any manager at any size or type of company can use the Identification and Justification Models to find the right information to begin tracking in real time and begin real-time opportunity detection.

It is a long way from these first steps in real-time opportunity detection to becoming a Real-Time Enterprise. It may take years for an organization to apply real-time opportunity detection to all its most critical business processes, much less to refine its ability to respond in all these processes. Certainly the transition can be eased if a corporation assigns one or more executives to take on the functions of long-distance lookout, Real-Time Enterprise change leader, and internal monitor and reporter, but it will be a difficult transition nonetheless. An integral part of the transition will be the slow process of managers and entire organizations learning to deal with present shock.

Present Shock

In 1970 Alvin Toffler coined the term *future shock,* meaning "the shattering stress and disorientation that we induce in individuals by subjecting them to too much change in too short a time."[1] Perhaps it is time to coin a new term, *present shock:* the difficulty in changing management and work styles to focus on the detection of events rather than reactions to them. *Present shock* specifically speaks to the existence of enormous amounts of information about the here and now and the need to develop well-honed and effective individual skills, tools, and corporatewide changes to organizational structures and managerial practices so that the power of the present can be harnessed and controlled.

It is perhaps difficult to understand why this change in business focus will be so challenging without considering the fact that during the tens of thousands of years of human history, it has only been in the last 175 that human beings have been able to have instantaneous knowledge of events occurring beyond the range of our sight and hearing. In 1844 Samuel Morse sent the first telegraph message forty miles between Baltimore and Washington and ushered in a new era of awareness of events beyond the horizon (the first message: "What hath God wrought?").[2] Before this seminal event, our limited ability to know what was occurring in the present limited human endeavors to simply responding to events that had already occurred. In short, as a species we recognized the limitations of our hearing and sight and molded most of our behavior toward responding to events rather than detecting events the moment they occur. Despite living in a world where we now routinely converse in real time with people on the other side of the country and watch sporting events live as they happen on the other side of the planet, we have not yet grasped the ability to change our most fundamental ways of thinking about detection of events and responding to them. Just as it took factories forty years to achieve productivity gains from electric motors, it will take us many years to truly grasp the power of the present.

Heads Up

I hope this book has provided you with a heads-up on the power of the present, the power of real-time information. Companies will be transformed and entire economies affected by the coming of real-time opportunity detection and Real-Time Enterprises, but the changes will begin only one manager at a time. Chapter 1 commented on the gains in material prosperity and prestige that await managers who implement real-time opportunity detection in their organizations. The first step to being such a manager is simply to ask: "Is there information about my customers, new trends, unforeseen opportunities, and so on that would make me change my current course of action?" Undoubtedly the answer is "Yes." If so, begin today with the Identification and Justification Models to determine what real-time information will benefit you the most and then pursue it.

While you read this book, managers around the world were beginning to use real-time information to improve business results. Ford has begun collecting real-time sales data to make micro-adjustments to prices for maximum profitability; pharmaceutical companies are more efficiently allocating research efforts as a result of early identification of promising drug compounds. On the other hand, the SARS epidemic (a surprise event) provided fresh evidence of the value of real-time information to both public health and to the economies of Asia and Toronto.

Real-time information will transform the business world. Managers will inevitably have to confront present shock—the only question now is when. Will you be one of those who leads through present shock (and reaps the benefits) starting today? Or will you wait—will the onset of present shock be a surprise or suspected event in your career? Heads up.

notes

Introduction

1. Keith C. Heidorn, "The 1900 Galveston Hurricane," <http://www.islandnet.com/~see/weather/events/1900hurr.htm> (accessed 17 September 2003).
2. Isaac M. Cline, "Special Report on the Galveston Hurricane of September 8, 1900," 23 September 1900, Available at <http://www.history.noaa.gov/tales/weather/cline2.html> (accessed 10 August 2002)
3. Assumptions: Beginning from a zero balance, $10,000 is invested each year for seven years; inflation is not taken into account in calculating investment amount or return. After seven years, no new money is invested. Assuming an average annual return of 8 percent (fairly standard in financial planning calculators), after seven years the savings balance would be $96,366. Under current market conditions, the sum would be more likely to be $60,000.
4. Many analysts will tell you, however, that the agreement reached has more than enough loopholes to allow investment banks to once again engage in the same behaviors that the settlement was supposed to stop.
5. Dell and Wal-Mart have been purposefully excluded from the book as examples. Years ago I heard author and humorist Calvin Trillin being interviewed on the radio. During the interview he said he once had given thought to starting a society of American historians whose members would pledge to never quote de Tocqueville. Likewise, in an effort to

bring a new perspective to the impact information technology is having on business, I would like to start a society of information technology research analysts whose members pledge never to use Dell or Wal-Mart in any of their research case studies. The two companies have been written about over and over again, and their methods and practices are well understood. I have deliberately used other examples to show that the principles of the Real-Time Enterprise apply and can be successfully implemented by companies of any size in any situation and are not the exclusive province of market-leading behemoths.

6. Following is an excerpt from "Report of the President's Commission on the Accident at Three Mile Island" (available at <http://stellarone.com/nuclear/index.htm>, accessed 11 November 2002):

> *In September 1977, an incident occurred at the Davis-Besse plant, also equipped with a B&W reactor. . . . A B&W engineer had stated in an internal B&W memorandum written more than a year before the TMI accident that if the Davis-Besse event had occurred in a reactor operating at full power, "it is quite possible, perhaps probable, that core uncovery and possible fuel damage would have occurred."*
>
> *He urged, in the strongest terms, that clear instructions be passed on to the operators. This memorandum was written thirteen months before the accident at Three Mile Island, but no new instructions resulted from it.*
>
> *An NRC official in January 1978 pointed out the likelihood for erroneous operator action in a TMI-type incident. The NRC did not notify utilities prior to the accident.*
>
> *A Tennessee Valley Authority (TVA) engineer analyzed the problem of rising pressurizer level and falling pressure more than a year before the accident. His analysis was provided to B&W, NRC, and the Advisory Committee on Reactor Safeguards. Again no notification was given to utilities prior to the accident.*

7. "Report of the President's Commission on the Accident at Three Mile Island."

8. Presidential Commission on the Space Shuttle *Challenger* Accident, "Report of the Presidential Commission on the Space Shuttle *Challenger* Accident, Chapter 4." Available at <http://science.ksc.nasa.gov/shuttle/missions/51-l/docs/rogers-commission/table-of-contents.html> (accessed 10 October 2002).

9. During a hearing on February 11, 1986, one of the commissioners, Nobel Laureate Richard Feynman, dipped an O ring into a vat of cold water. After leaving the ring in the water for just a few minutes, Dr. Feynman squeezed the ring and clearly demonstrated how exposure to the cold had rendered the ring nonpliable and therefore made disaster certain if the shuttle launched in temperatures below 53 degrees Fahrenheit (see Andrew J. Dunar and Stephen P. Waring, *Power to Explore: A History of Marshall Space Flight Center, 1960–1990* (Washington, DC: GPO, 1999), 392, <http://history.msfc.nasa.gov/book/chptten.pdf>). The commission also stated in Chapter 5:

> *The decision to launch the* Challenger *was flawed. Those who made that decision were unaware of the recent history of problems concerning the O-rings and the joint and were unaware of the initial written recommendation of the contractor advising against the launch at temperatures below 53 degrees Fahrenheit and the continuing opposition of the engineers at Thiokol after the management reversed its position. They did not have a clear understanding of Rockwell's concern that it was not safe to launch because of ice on the pad.*

10. "Report of the Presidential Commission on the Space Shuttle *Challenger* Accident, Chapter 5."

11. U.S. Senate Select Committee on Intelligence and the U.S. House of Representatives Permanent Select Committee on Intelligence, "Findings of the Final Report of the Senate Select Committee on Intelligence and the House Permanent Select Committee on Intelligence Joint Inquiry into the Terrorist Attacks of September 11, 2001," available at <http://intelligence.senate.gov/pubs107.htm> (accessed 1 August 2003).

12. Tom Topolinski, senior analyst, Gartner Dataquest, telephone interview by author, 20 November 2002.

Chapter 1

1. American Institute of Physics and David Cassidy, "Heisenberg— Quantum Mechanics, 1925–1927: The Uncertainty Principle," <http://www.aip.org/history/heisenberg/p08.htm> (accessed 19 June 2003).

2. Boise State University, "Mount Saint Helens Volcanic Eruption," <http://www.boisestate.edu/history/ncasner/hy210/volcano.htm>

(accessed 19 June 2003); Incorporated Research Institutions for Seismology, "NOAA Images—The Eruption of Mount Saint Helens," <http://www.iris.washington.edu/EandO/slidescans/sthelens/slideshow/index.htm> (accessed 19 June 2003); Dick Thompson, *Volcano Cowboys: The Rocky Evolution of a Dangerous Science* (New York: St. Martin's Press, 2000), 90–91.

3. Svenska Ostindiska Companiet, "The Story of the East Indiaman *Gothenburg*," East Indiaman *Gothenburg* Museum, Gothenburg, Sweden (visited 12 April 2002). Also see Anders Wästfelt, "The Marine Archaeological Excavation of the East Indiaman *Götheborg*," <http://www.gotheborg.com/essays/awmarex.shtml> (accessed 12 December 2002), and B. Allenström, M. Brown and J. Lundgren, "An East Indiaman Ship and Its Safety," <www.sname.org/AM2001/paper3.pdf> (accessed 12 December 2002).

4. Sharon Brownlee, "Early-Detection Revisionism," *New York Times Magazine*, 15 December 2002, 84.

5. U.S. Department of Defense Security Institute, "An Assessment of the Aldrich H. Ames Espionage Case and Its Implications for U.S. Intelligence," report of the Staff of the Senate Select Committee on Intelligence, Sen. Print 103-90, 103d Cong. 2d Sess. 51 (1994). Edited version available at <http://www.loyola.edu/dept/politics/intel/sab4.html> (accessed 9 December 2002).

6. "Summary of the Hayman Fire, Colorado," August 23, 2002, <http://www.wildfirecentral.org/facts/photouploads/20021008155032-24268.pdf> (accessed 19 March 2003).

7. U.S. District Court, District of Colorado, *United States* v. *Terry Barton*, Attachment B, June 16, 2002.

8. "Hayman Fire Info," Hayman Fire Rehab and Recovery, <http://www.uppersouthplatte.org/hayman_info.htm> (accessed 16 March 2003).

Chapter 2

1. Richard Morenus, *DEW Line: Distant Early Warning, the Miracle of America's First Line of Defense* (New York: Rand McNally, 1957).

2. Requirements for effective metrics based on Robert Eccles et al., *Value Reporting Revolution: Moving Beyond the Earnings Game* (New York: Wiley, 2001), 20–21.

3. Robert S. Kaplan and David P. Norton, "The Balanced Scorecard: Measures that Drive Performance," *Harvard Business Review*, January–February 1992, 71–79; Robert S. Kaplan and David P. Norton,

The Balanced Scorecard: Translating Strategy into Action (Boston: Harvard Business School Press, 1996), 8.

4. Financial Accounting Standards Board, "Qualitative Characteristics of Accounting Information," *Statement of Financial Accounting Concepts*, No. 2, Section AU 312.10.

Chapter 3

1. Loyola University Political Science Department, ed., "An Assessment of the Aldrich H. Ames Espionage Case and Its Implications for U.S. Intelligence," <http://www.loyola.edu/dept/politics/intel/sab4.html> (accessed 9 December 2002).
2. Ibid.
3. Ibid.
4. Greg Rayburn, interview by author, Ashburn, VA, 6 November 2002. Rayburn was a certified public accountant, certified fraud examiner, and a member of the Turnaround Management Association, the American Institute of Public Accountants, and the American Bankruptcy Institute.
5. Like most other communications carriers, from time to time World-Com would use the network facilities of other third-party carriers to serve its customers. The fees paid by WorldCom to these carriers are called *line costs*.
6. Arthur Levitt, "The Numbers Game" (speech delivered at the New York University Center for Law and Business, New York, 28 September 1998). Available at http://www.sed.gov/news/speech/speecharchive/1998/spch220.txt (accessed 17 October 2002). Levitt was former chairman of the Securities and Exchange Commission.
7. Bernard Ebbers, "MCI Worldcom" (speech delivered at National Press Club, Washington DC, 12 January 2000). Ebbers was president and CEO of MCI Worldcom.
8. Paul Becket, "National Century Trouble Was Longstanding," *Wall Street Journal*, 21 November 2002; Edward Iwata, "National's Downfall Came Two Years After Signs Surfaced," *USA Today*, 24 November 2002; Jackie Spinner, "Healthcare Receivables Trade Grows: Uncertain Payment Process Expands Risk," *Washington Post*, 25 December 2002. Due to company policies and/or pending lawsuits, National Century Financial Enterprises, Bank One, JP Morgan Chase, and CSFB declined to speak with us on the record.
9. Michael Gregory, "NCFE Suit Targets Practically Everyone," asset securitization report, 2 June 2003.

10. Becket, "National Century Trouble Was Longstanding."

11. Whether driven by the NCFE scandal or not, Bank One sold its corporate trust business in July 2003. Mike Pramik, "Chicago-Based Bank One to Sell Corporate Trust Business," *Columbus Dispatch*, 25 July 2003.

12. "United Pilot Contract Could Be Most Expensive Ever," *Reuters News*, 28 August 2000.

13. "United Airlines Contract with Machinists and Ramp Workers Still to Come," *Airline Industry Information*, 29 August 2000; "Tentative Agreement Reached in United Airlines Strike," *United Press International*, 28 August 2000.

14. Patricia Richardson, "Dogfight at UAL; Pilot Chief Outmaneuvers CEO in Showdown," *Crain's Chicago Business*, 28 August 2000, 1.

15. Mark Pilling, "Labour Peace Comes with a High Price Tag at Delta," *Airline Business*, May 2001, 15; Barbara Cook and David Jonas, "Delta, Pilots Tentatively Agree, Labor Issues Loom Large," *Business Travel News*, 7 May 2001, 12.

16. Steve Wilhelm, "Boeing Positioned for Strong, Profitable 2001," *Puget Sound Business Journal*, 29 December 2000, 14.

17. Leo Mullin (prepared remarks presented at Delta Air Lines, Inc., 2001 Annual Shareowners' Meeting, 26 April 2001), <http://www.delta.com/docs/lfmannual01.doc> (accessed 26 November 2002). Also available through Delta's Investor Relations Department. Mullin is CEO of Delta Airlines.

18. Eric Amel, telephone interview by author, tape recording, 25 October 2002.

Chapter 4

1. Malcolm Gladwell, *The Tipping Point: How Little Things Can Make a Big Difference* (Boston: Little Brown, 2000), 30–33.

2. Mary Flood, "VP's Memo: 'Has Enron Become a Risky Place?'" *Houston Chronicle*, 16 January 2002.

3. Boeing 10K Report, 1995, <http://www.sec.gov/Archives/edgar/data/12927/0000012927-96-000003.txt> (accessed 28 December 2002), 23. Due to company policies regarding settled lawsuits, Boeing declined to speak with us on the record.

4. Stanley Holmes and Mike France, "Boeing's Secret," *Business Week*, 20 May 2002.

5. Boeing, "Boeing Reports 1997 3rd Quarter Results," 24 October 1997, <http://www.boeing.com/news/releases/1997/news_release_971024a.html> (accessed 29 December 2002).

6. Neil Bennett, "Business Profile: Boeing's Top Gun," *Daily Telegraph*, 29 July 2001.

7. Chuck Taylor, "Streamlining Contributed to Supply Snafus," *Seattle Times*, 26 October 1997.

8. Stanley Holmes, "Boeing Risk Backfired Last Week," *Seattle Times*, 26 October 1997.

9. Ibid.

10. Holmes and France, "Boeing's Secret."

11. Ibid.

12. Taylor, "Streamlining Contributed to Supply Snafus."

13. Ibid.

14. The facts of Boeing's production problems and its announced losses were contested in a class action lawsuit filed by some Boeing share-holders. The lawsuit alleged that Boeing withheld information about the production problems and did not properly report costs related to the problems. Boeing settled the suit while disputing the claims of the suit. In a statement to *Business Week*, Boeing's spokesperson said that Boeing had decided to settle because it was hesitant to try a case involving complex accounting issues in front of a Seattle jury after it had announced it was moving its headquarters out of Washington.

15. "Jobs Behind Schedule Chart," Decision on motion to dismiss Case No. C97-1715Z Class Action Order, *Francine Werbowsky and Mary Jane Howard, on behalf of themselves and all others similarly situated, Plaintiff*, v. *The Boeing Company, Philip M. Condit, Ronald Wood-ward and Boyd E. Givan*, United States District Court, Western District of Washington, Seattle filed 8 September 1998. Available at <http://securities.stanford.edu/1012/BA97/order.html> (accessed 15 February 2003).

16. For a full discussion of contingent road maps see Hugh Courtney, *20/20 Foresight: Crafting Strategy in an Uncertain World* (Boston: Harvard Business School Press, 2001).

17. Robert Berner and Heather Timmons, "Sears: A Slippery Slope Made of Plastic," *Business Week*, 6 May 2002. Due to company poli-cies and/or pending lawsuits, Sears declined to speak with us on the record.

18. Robert Berner, "Sears: A Horse Race for the Top Job," *Business Week*, 10 July 2000.

19. Robert Berner, "How Plastic Put Sears in a Pickle," *Business Week*, 30 October 2002; Berner and Timmons, "Sears."

20. Joe Hallinan and Amy Merrick, "Credit Cards Swipe Sears Profits," *Wall Street Journal*, 11 February 2003.

21. Constance L. Hayes, "A Bet on Credit Cards Becomes Messy at Sears," *New York Times,* 10 November 2002.

22. Kevin Keleghan has filed suit against Alan Lacy and Sears alleging that Mr. Lacy's comments defamed him and "raised the false question of whether Keleghan is fit to serve in any position of trust in any executive capacity in any business where shareholder interests are at stake." *Kevin T. Keleghan v. Sears, Roebuck and Co. and Alan J. Lacy.* Case No. 02L938, Lake County (Ill.) Circuit Court, filed 18 November 2002.

23. Hallinan and Merrick, "Credit Cards Swipe Sears Profits."

24. Robin Sidell, Amy Merrick, and Joe Hallinan, "Sears Plans to Sell Credit Card Unit in Major Change," *Wall Street Journal,* 26 March 2003; Dina ElBoghdady and Caroline Mayer, "Citigroup to Buy Sears Credit Unit; Retailer to Shift Focus with $3 Billion Sale," *Washington Post,* 16 July 2003.

Chapter 5

1. Karen L. Burcham and Alexander E. Smith, "Precision Landing Systems" (paper presented at the Air Traffic Control Association Proceedings, Arlington, VA, 30 September–3 October 1991), 3, <http://www.rannoch.com/PDF/precision.pdf> (accessed 10 January 2003).

2. Alan Staats, "Thwarting Skyjackings from the Ground," FACSNET, <http://www.facsnet.org/issues/specials/terrorism/aviation.php3> (accessed 10 January 2003).

3. "We will invest in new technology for aircraft security, with grants to develop transponders that cannot be switched off from the cockpit; video monitors in the cockpit to alert pilots to trouble in the cabin—and we will look at all kinds of technologies to make sure that our airlines are safe—and for example, including technology to enable controllers to take over distressed aircraft and land it by remote control." George W. Bush, "At O'Hare, President Says 'Get On Board'" (remarks by the President to airline employees, O'Hare International Airport, Chicago, 27 September 2001), <http://www.whitehouse.gov/news/releases/2001/09/20010927-1.html> (accessed 11 January 2003).

4. Alan Greenspan, "Economic Volatility," speech at symposium sponsored by the Federal Reserve Bank of Kansas City, Jackson Hole, Wyoming, 30 August 2002, <http://www.federalreserve.gov/boarddocs/speeches/2002/20020830/default.htm>

5. Mike Farrar and Dan Johnson, telephone interview by author, 24 February 2003. Farrar was vice president of marketing and Johnson was vice president of construction for Amberwood Homes. Subsequent quotations of Farrar and Johnson are from this interview.

6. Amberwood Homes is a privately held company and does not discuss financial results.

7. Ron Hunt and Michael Relich, telephone interview by author, 7 March 2003. Hunt was operations manager and Relich was chief information officer, Wet Seal, Inc. Subsequent quotations of Hunt and Relich are from this interview.

8. Relich noted that a similar system had been considered in the past; the speed of dial-up connections would not have enabled the volume of information required to be transmitted. "Given what we could transmit on dial-up the $20/month average cost of a line couldn't be justified. On the other hand, the bandwidth we get with DSL allows us to transmit large volumes of data for our reports which easily justifies the $40/month it costs."

9. Norihiko Shirouzu, "Under the Hood: At Ford, Revamp Means Rebuilding a Wrecked System," *Wall Street Journal,* 17 October 2003; "Ford Runs 20% Ahead of Targets to Reduce Its Per-Vehicle Costs," *Wall Street Journal,* 17 September 2002; Jamie Butters, "Ford Sees Expense, Job Cut Goals Met," *Detroit Free Press,* 17 September 2002; Jamie Butters, "At Ford: Cut Costs or Else," *Detroit Free Press,* 22 September 2002; Betsy Morris, "Can Ford Save Ford?" *Fortune,* 18 November 2002, 52.

10. Dresdner Kleinwort Wasserstein is the investment banking division of Dresdner Bank, a subsidiary of the Allianz Group. Dresdner's real-time risk management system is similar to those used by a number of financial services firms.

11. Michael Crouhy, Dan Galai, and Robert Mark, *Risk Management* (New York: McGraw Hill, 2001), 1–41.

12. "Derivative product: Typically an instrument that is created (derived) through a combination of cash market instruments. They may be equity, commodity, interest or currency based." Robert J. Schwartz and Clifford W. Smith, Jr., eds., *Derivatives Handbook, Risk Management and Control* (New York: Wiley, 1997), 634.

13. Bank of England, "Extract from the Conclusion of the Bank of England Report on the Collapse of Barings," *Bank of England Report on Barings,* Section 13.6, available at <http://www.numa.com/ref/barings/bar02.htm> (accessed 15 January 2003).

14. I would like to thank my colleague Mary Knox for a research note that led me to Dresdner, "Real-Time Risk Management and

Capital Allocation," Case Studies CS-18-0958, Gartner, Inc., 2002.

15. Louise Beeson and Karen Laureno-Rikardsen, telephone interview by author, tape recording, 7 January 2003.

16. B. J. Hodge, Willam P. Anthony, and Lawrence M. Gales, *Organizational Theory: A Strategic Approach* (Upper Saddle River, NJ: Prentice Hall, 1996), 60.

17. eBay, Inc., "Our Mission," *Company Overview*, <http://pages. ebay.com/community/aboutebay/overview/index.html> (accessed 10 January 2003).

18. :n/e/tsurf, "Items Sold On eBay Which Made Headline News," <http://www.netsurf.ch/ebaywatch.html> (accessed 10 January 2003).

19. Eric Young, "eBay to Ban All Hate-Related Items," *Industry Standard,* 3 May 2001; eBay, Inc., "eBay Revises Listing Policy: Expanded Policy Bans Most Historical Artifacts Associated with Nazi Germany and Hate Groups," eBay news release, 3 May 2001, <http://www.shareholder.com/ebay/news/20010503-40497.htm> (accessed 10 January 2003); eBay, Inc., "Human Parts and Remains," *eBay Selling Policies,* <http://pages.ebay.com/ help/community/png-remains.html> (accessed 10 January 2003).

20. Ron Harris, "Elian for Auction," Associated Press, 28 April 2000.

21. :n/e/tsurf, "Items Sold on eBay Which Made Headline News."

22. Ibid.

23. Ibid.

24. "*Columbia* Timeline to Disaster," *Sky News*, <http://uk.news. yahoo.com/030202/140/dqm5b.html> (accessed 6 February 2003).

25. Maynard Webb, interview by author, tape recording, San Jose, CA, 23 May 2002. Webb was CIO of eBay, Inc.

Part 3

1. P. A. David, "Computer and Dynamo: The Modern Productivity Paradox in a Not-Too-Distant Mirror" (Stanford, CA: Center for Economic Policy Research, 1989).

Chapter 6

1. David A. Bosnich, "The Principle of Subsidiarity," *Journal of Religion and Liberty* 6, no. 8 (1996), <http://www.acton.org/publi-cat/randl/article.php?id=200> (accessed 12 February 2003).

2. CEO, CFO, and COO of Audio Inc., telephone interview by author, 11 November 2002.

3. General Motors, Inc., "Pension Review with Security Analysts and Media," 20 August 2002, <http://www.gm.com/company/investor_information/docs/presentations/pension_8_20_2002.pdf> (accessed 16 February 2003).

4. David Welch and Kathleen Kerwin, "Rick Wagoner's Game Plan" *Business Week,* 10 February 2003, 5260.

5. Randy Williams, "Headshot: GM's G. Richard Wagoner, GM's New Forward, Defends Against Market Share Slide," *Hoover's Online,* 25 July 2000, <http://www.hoovers.com/features/headshot.html> (accessed 10 February 2003).

6. G. Richard Wagoner, interview by author, tape recording, Detroit, MI, 14 February 2003. Wagoner was president, CEO, and chairman-elect of General Motors.

7. Pat Morrissey, interview by author, tape recording, Detroit, MI, 5 March 2003. Morrissey was director of manufacturing communications of General Motors. Subsequent Morrissey quotations are from this interview.

8. The three stages in which GM measures quality are "final line," "dynamic vehicle testing," and "CARE line."

9. Gary Cowger, interview by author, tape recording, Detroit, MI, 24 February 2003. Cowger was president of GM North America. Subsequent Cowger quotations are from this interview.

10. Dustin Braun et al., "Toyota Motor Manufacturing," <http://legacy.csom.umn.edu/CNFiles/CM/Fal2002/62_Toyota_Presentation.ppt> (accessed 7 March 2003).

11. Welch and Kerwin, "Rick Wagoner's Game Plan."

12. Wagoner, interview by author.

13. "A new organizational structure for GM's North American passenger car operations is formed. Two integrated car groups, Chevrolet, Pontiac, GM of Canada (C-P-C) and Buick, Oldsmobile, Cadillac (B-O-C), each have complete responsibility for their respective products, including engineering, manufacturing, assembly and marketing," General Motors, *Corporate History, 1984,* <http://www.gm.com/company/corp_info/history/gmhis1980.html> (accessed 7 March 2003).

14. Wagoner, interview by author.

15. Jerry Elson, interview by author, tape recording, Detroit, MI, 5 February 2002. Elson was GM vice president of vehicle operations in North America. Subsequent Elson quotations are from this interview.

16. James Queen, interview by author, tape recording, Detroit, MI, 6 February 2003. Queen was GM vice president of North America engineering. Subsequent Queen quotations are from this interview.

17. Wagoner, interview by author.

18. General Electric, "Cultural Change Process," <http://www.ge.com/en/company/news/culture.htm> (accessed 6 March 2003).

19. Wagoner, interview by author.

20. Harbour Inc., "The 2002 Harbour Report," <http://www.harbourinc.com> (accessed 8 February 2003).

21. Wagoner, interview by author.

Chapter 7

1. Horst Kohler, "The Challenges of Globalization and the Role of the IMF" (paper presented at the Annual Meeting of the Society for Economics and Management, Humboldt University, Berlin, Germany, 15 May 2003). Available at <http://www.imf.org/external/np/speeches/2003/051503.htm> (accessed 22 July 2003). Kohler was managing director of the International Monetary Fund.

2. Stanley Fischer, "The Asian Crisis: A View from the IMF" (paper presented at Midwinter Conference of the Bankers' Association for Foreign Trade, Washington, DC, 22 January 1998). Available at <http://www.imf/org/external/np/speeches/1998/012298.htm> (accessed 18 November 2002). Fischer was first deputy managing director of the International Monetary Fund.

3. Jerry Elson, telephone interview by author, 5 February 2002. Elson was vice president of GM's North American vehicle operations.

4. Valerie Alvord, "L.A. Latest City to Fight Against False Alarms; Rule Requires Alarm Companies to Verify Crime Before Calling Police," *USA Today,* 21 February 2003.

5. Ron Hunt, telephone interview by author, 9 February 2003. Hunt was operations manager of Wet Seal, Inc.

6. Portions drawn from Carol Rozwell, "Real Time Takes Time: Reshaping Attitudes and Behaviors," Report Number COM-14-7138, Gartner Inc., 28 November 2001.

7. Alan Greenspan, "Aging Global Population," testimony before the U.S. Senate Special Committee on Aging, Washington, DC, 27 February 2003.

8. *Wall Street Journal,* 28 February 2003, C1.

9. Hunt, interview by author.

10. C. K. Prahalad and Gary Hamel, "The Core Competence of the Corporation," *Harvard Business Review,* May–June 1990.

11. Ken McGee, "Aging Populations Pose Opportunities and Problems," GartnerG2 report, 21 September 2001.

12. Rebecca Blumenstein, Joann S. Lublin, and Shawn Young, "Sprint Forced Out Top Executives over Questionable Tax Shelter," *Wall Street Journal,* 5 February 2003; Laurie P. Cohen, Kate Kelly and Deborah Solomon, "NYSE's Reed Scraps Report, Plans New One— A Top-to-Bottom Examination Is Set of Exchange's Governance; Lead Director McCall Resigns," *Wall Street Journal,* 26 September 2003, C1.

13. Louis Lavelle, "Rebuilding Trust in Tyco," *Business Week,* 25 November 2002.

14. Price Waterhouse Financial and Cost Management Team, *CFO: Architect of the Corporation's Future* (New York: Wiley, 1997), 15–23.

15. In 1968 German operations researcher Dietrich Braess empirically showed how increasing capacity in a component of a process could actually slow down the overall desired result, even if the subsequent steps in the process appeared to be able to accommodate the increased load. See Thomas Bass, "Road to Ruin," *Discover,* May 1992, 1.

16. Clearly the analogy is less than perfect, but it is useful. Note that the third position in the scheme of checks and balances is held by the Supreme Court in both cases: in government the court rules on the constitutionality of actions of both the executive and legislative branches, and in business it represents the rule of law.

17. U.S. General Accounting Office, <www.gao.gov> (accessed 12 March 2003). Note that the General Accounting Office, as of fall 2003, is studying a proposal to generate a set of national performance indicators for the United States. While there is no mention of monitoring these indicators in real time as yet, clearly the GAO is mirroring the CMO role in this respect. See <www.gao.gov/npi>.

18. Sherron Watkins, "Opening Statement" (presented before the U.S. House of Representatives Committee on Energy and Commerce, Subcommittee on Oversight and Investigations, Washington, DC, 14 February 2002). Jeffrey Skilling was CEO and Andrew Fastow was CFO of Enron when Ms. Watkins noticed that there were substantial irregularities in the way the company was handling its partnerships.

19. Sarbanes-Oxley Act (Pub. L. No. 107-204, 116 Stat. 745), Section 806, amended 18 U.S.C. § 1514 A to provide protection for whistleblowers.

20. Michael Useem, telephone interview by author, 11 July 2003.

21. Lavelle, "Rebuilding Trust in Tyco."

22. See, for instance, the Wall Street Journal's special Corporate Governance section, 24 February 2003.

Chapter 8

1. PricewaterhouseCoopers, "Fifth Annual Global CEO Survey: Uncertain Times, Abundant Opportunities," 2001, <http://www.pwcglobal. com/gx/eng/ins-sol/surveyrep/ceo/PwC_Global_CEO_Survey.pdf> (accessed 17 October 2002).

2. Michael Relich, telephone interview by author, 7 March 2003. Relich was CIO of Wet Seal, Inc.

3. The chart also shows that the rise in IT spending was responsible for most of the growth in capital investments by business during the expansion.

4. Relich, interview by author.

5. Marianne Kobalsuk McGee, "Better Data, Better Decisions?" *Information Week,* 16 September 2002, 48.

6. Dan Johnson, telephone interview by author, 24 February 2003. Johnson was vice president of construction for Amberwood Homes.

7. See Sections 141(a) and 122(5) of the Delaware General Corporation Law, Delaware Code Annotated Title 8, available at <http://www.delcode.state.de.us> (accessed 16 May 2003).

8. *Malone* v. *Brincat,* 722 A.2d 5 (Del. 1998).

9. "General Corporations," <http://www.theincorporators.com/ corp_general.html> (accessed 12 February 2003).

10. See Section 141(e) of the Delaware General Corporation Law, Delaware Code Annotated Title 8, available at <http://www.delcode. state.de.us> (accessed 16 May 2003).

11. "General Coporations."

12. Ty R. Sagalow, "Directors and Officers Liability Insurance," *The Directors Handbook Series* (Deerfield, Illinois: National Association of Corporate Directors, 1999).

13. An insurance industry standard definition of a wrongful act is "any actual or alleged act, error, omission, misstatement, misleading statement or breach of duty by an insured person in his or her capacity as a director or officer of the company." Excerpted from a specimen of a directors' and officers' insurance policy from Kemper Insurance Companies.

14. Business Cycle Dating Committee, "The Business-Cycle Peak of March 2001," National Bureau of Economic Research, Washington, DC, 26 November 2001.

15. Bureau of Economic Analysis, "National Income and Product Accounts Second Quarter 2002 GDP (Advance) Revised Estimates: 1999 Through First Quarter 2002," U.S. Department of Commerce, 31 July 2002.

16. Securities and Exchange Commission, "Quarterly Reports on Form 10-Q and Form 10-QSB," *Rule 13a-13* (17 CFR 240.13a-13):

> *Except as provided in paragraphs (b) and (c) of this section, every issuer that has securities registered pursuant to section 12 of the Act and is required to file annual reports pursuant to section 13 of the Act, and has filed or intends to file such reports on Form 10-K and Form 10-KSB or U5S, shall file a quarterly report on Form 10-Q and Form 10-QSB within the period specified in General Instruction A.1. to that form for each of the first three quarters of each fiscal year of the issuer, commencing with the first fiscal quarter following the most recent fiscal year for which full financial statements were included in the registration statement, or, if the registration statement included financial statements for an interim period subsequent to the most recent fiscal year end meeting the requirements of Article 10 of Regulation S-X, for the first fiscal quarter subsequent to the quarter reported upon in the registration statement.*

17. Current rules call for filings to be submitted within fifteen calendar days after the occurrence of the following events: (1) changes in control of registrant, (2) acquisition or disposition of assets, and (3) bankruptcy or receivership. Submission within five calendar days is required in the case of the following events: (1) changes in registrant's certifying accountant or (2) resignations of registrant's directors. See general instructions on A. Rule as to Use of Form 8-K and B. Securities and Exchange Commission, "Events to be Reported and Time for Filing of Reports," Washington, DC: Securities and Exchange Commission. Available at <http://www.sec.gov/divisions/corpfin/forms/8-k.htm> (accessed 9 June 2003).

18. Securities and Exchange Commission, "Rule as to the Use of Form 10Q" (Washington, DC: Securities and Exchange Commission. Available at <http://www4.law.cornell.edu/uscode/15/78m.html> (accessed 9 June 2003). Securities and Exchange Commission, "Rule as to the Use of Form 10K" (Washington, D.C.: Securities and Exchange Commission. Available at <http://www4.law.cornell.edu/uscode/15/78m.html> (accessed 9 June 2003).

19. Securities and Exchange Commission, "SEC to Propose New Corporate Disclosure Rules," press release (Washington, DC, 13 February 2002).
20. The current inexorable moves toward expensing of options and appointing a minimum number of independent directors provide useful examples of market forces compelling compliance once the first announcement has been made.

Conclusion

1. Alvin Toffler, *Future Shock* (New York: Random House, 1970), 2.
2. Mary Bellis, "The History of the Telegraph," Inventors at About.com, <http://inventors.about.com/library/inventors/bltelegraph.htm> (accessed 15 March 2003).

index

about the author

KENNETH G. MCGEE is group vice president and re-search fellow at Gartner, Inc., a research and advisory firm specializing in information technology and business growth. McGee has been with Gartner since 1989 and is currently conducting research in a new area, the Real-Time Enterprise. He also focuses on how IT will influence societal, government, and economic forces that will in turn fundamentally shift business organizational and management practices. In his previous work at Gartner he served as Gartner's senior analyst covering global network services providers, network organizations, and network outsourcing. Prior to joining Gartner, McGee was vice president and director of international telecommunications for Salomon Brothers and was based in London, England. He has also held senior IT management positions at Citicorp North American Investment Bank and Goldman, Sachs & Co.